IN RODIN'S
STUDIO

ALBERT E. ELSEN

Walter A. Haas Professor of Art History, Stanford University

IN RODIN'S STUDIO

A photographic record of sculpture in the making

PHAIDON

in association with the Musée Rodin

Phaidon Press Limited, Littlegate House,
St Ebbe's Street, Oxford, in association
with the Musée Rodin, Paris

First published 1980
© 1980 Albert E. Elsen
All rights reserved

ISBN 0 7148 1976 X

Printed in Great Britain by Jolly & Barber Ltd, Rugby, England
Origination of illustrations by Bussière Arts Graphiques, Paris

Contents

Acknowledgements

That scholars today talk about a new era of Rodin scholarship is due to the administration of Madame Monique Laurent, Curator of the Musée Rodin, and Jean Chatelain, member of the museum's Conseil d'Administration. For the first time responsible art historians have been given access to the important archives of the Musée Rodin. In 1977, my wife and I were shown the museum's great photographic collection. This publication is a collaborative effort between the author and the museum, whose intention it is to draw attention to a neglected and invaluable resource for the understanding of Rodin's art. Our confidence in the quality of the Phaidon Press inspired its selection as publisher. My purpose in this book has been to focus upon what these photographs tell us about Rodin's art and his relation to photography and photographers. The archival research of Patricia Elsen was crucial to the finding and identifying of several previously unknown works, and she did invaluable editorial work on the text and catalogue. Professor Kirk Varnedoe of Columbia University, who will publish on several of the photographers who worked for Rodin and the importance of the photographs for Rodin's drawings and changing views of his own sculpture, gave fully of his knowledge and time to this enterprise. His suggestions and those of my colleague Lorenz Eitner regarding the manuscript were greatly appreciated. I am indebted to Maria Morris, a graduate student at Columbia University, for her identification of the types of photographic prints. Others who generously shared their knowledge of photography were Kit Monroe and Stanford colleagues, Anita Mozley and Leo Holub. Much of the pleasure of working on this project came from the spirited assistance of the Musée Rodin staff, Mademoiselle Claudie Jourdrin, Madame Lucette Proste and Madame Helène Pinet. Thanks are due also to Professor Daniel Rosenfeld of Boston University for supplying names and dates for many of the marble sculptures. The author and the publisher wish the contribution of their late colleague, Keith Roberts, to be recognized, for it was he who initiated the idea for this publication. Finally, this book is dedicated to Mr B. Gerald Cantor, whose enthusiasm and support for Rodin for so many years have greatly benefited the Musée Rodin in Paris and the Stanford University Art Museum.

Albert E. Elsen, Stanford, California 1979

Preface

Rodin's reputation rests, without doubt, on his sculpture, and it is to see and admire these works above all that visitors come to the Rodin Museum in Paris. However, Rodin was not merely a sculptor, and the extensive bequest made by him to the French State in 1916 included, apart from material from his studio – studies, sketches, models, and numerous plaster casts and terracottas – a great many other treasures: a collection of over 7,000 drawings, which has not yet been studied in detail and which is particularly interesting since, for the most part, the drawings bear no relation to Rodin's sculptures, and hence represent an entirely different aspect of Rodin's oeuvre; a number of collections including several thousand objects from Greece, Rome, Egypt, China, Japan and India. Admittedly, a large proportion of the items are not particularly significant or of outstanding quality, but taken together they show Rodin's great artistic curiosity.

Creator and collector, Rodin was also a man of his time and he bought, or was given, paintings and sculptures by the artists of his day: he kept, too, all his correspondence – the letters he received, drafts of those he sent – and a large collection of photographs.

The whole collection was given to the French State on the understanding that it would be housed in two museums: one at Meudon, Rodin's home, and a larger one in Paris, the Hôtel Biron, a fine eighteenth-century building which Rodin in fact never owned (as is often thought), but which was loaned to him by the State during the last years of his life.

The Rodin Museum, created in accordance with the terms of the bequest, has, naturally, undertaken the preservation of the collection. Moreover, for several years now, it has sought to make it more widely known and has encouraged further research (though it must not be forgotten that the Museum was not set up until 1919 and that the Second World War, 20 years later, interrupted such research).

The drawings have been classified according to the techniques appropriate to the medium, and a specialized reference collection will be put together in the not too distant future; exhibitions on different themes are now being organized systematically, to display hitherto little-known and unpublished sculptures and drawings; the archive material has been classified and filed.

The preserving and cataloguing of several tens of thousands of objects of different sizes, media and techniques clearly represents a vast undertaking. While it is the prime concern of the Museum to account for, and organize, the collection, this does not mean that the Rodin Museum wishes to have a monopoly over it – on the contrary, it is glad to have the collaboration of researchers from France and from abroad.

It is in this spirit of co-operation that the present edition of old photographs from the Museum archives has been compiled. Many were taken by great photographers at the end of the nineteenth and the beginning of the twentieth century. They have been selected by

Professor Albert Elsen of Stanford University, California, who has for many years been a Rodin specialist of unquestioned authority in the United States. At his request the publication of this work has been entrusted to Phaidon Press, Oxford, with the Museum taking the French language edition. The above observations will surely be sufficient to justify this international co-operation, which Rodin himself would doubtless have welcomed, since he hoped to see his work known abroad as well as in France.

Furthermore, this internationalism is fundamental to the nature of art itself, since art is the language common to all peoples. In the case of Rodin this is borne out daily by visitors from all the world over who come to the Museum that bears his name to admire there all he created, collected and loved.

The Musée Rodin

Introduction

Rodin

FRANÇOIS-AUGUSTE-RENÉ RODIN made his public début as a maker of statues in 1877, when his life was almost half over. Born of a lower-middle-class family in Paris in 1840, Rodin had little formal education, prompting one distinguished art historian to categorize him mistakenly as 'ignorant'. Artistically, his formal training was limited to attendance at the École des Dessins from 1854 to 1857, during which time he distinguished himself in drawing under the tutelage of Horace Lecoq de Boisbaudran and also discovered modelling. Three times he failed the entrance examinations for the École des Beaux-Arts, because his eighteenth-century modelling style was not in favour with the jurors. Resigned to supporting himself as a decorative artist, from 1857 until 1882 he worked largely for other artists. They signed their names to his work, as was customary and as Rodin was to do with the work of his own assistants. From the mid-1870s, despite his poverty, he managed to employ at least one assistant to help him on his own work. The upheaval of the Franco-Prussian War and the Commune made employment so difficult that Rodin was obliged to support himself, his mistress, Rose Beuret, and their son, Auguste, by working in Belgium from 1871 until 1877. A trip in 1875 to Italy, where he saw the work of Michelangelo, Donatello, and others, was crucial to his development and his determination to be a maker of statues. After his controversial début in the Paris Spring Salon of 1877 with his statue *The Age of Bronze*, he returned permanently to Paris.

Rodin's self-education as a sculptor was helped in part by contact with the sculptors who employed him, and also by contact with fellow decorative artists. In his own time this man of prodigious energy haunted the Louvre and the Salons and formed his own style from exposure to the works of Second Empire and early Third Republic sculptors, such as Jean-Baptiste Carpeaux (1827–75). By the time he was thirty, Rodin's hands were famous among his fellow workers not only for their speed and dexterity, but for their ability to fashion work in a variety of styles. Later in life he would complain of bad habits he had acquired from the type of work he had had to do: ornament designs, ceramic decoration, architectural reliefs, and *objets d'art*; but he also developed a lifelong love of *métier*. His signature style of working directly from the model was formed early with the *Mask of the Man with the Broken Nose*, which was rejected for exhibition in 1869, although its marble version was accepted in 1875.

Rodin's reputation as a great artist and his financial independence initially derived from portraits made in the 1880s. He began exhibiting internationally in the 1870s, but it was after 1880 that he was *invited* to show all over Europe. Contrary to the popular notion that Rodin was ignored or rejected by the French government, many of his works were bought by the Ministry of Fine Arts; and as early as the late 1870s, he began to make lifelong friends among influential politicians, who furthered his career. Within three years of his exhibition of *The Age of Bronze*, he received the first of several major commissions, *The Gates of Hell*, and during the following twenty years he produced monumental public sculptures that included *The Burghers of Calais* and the monuments to Claude Lorrain and Balzac. Thereafter, his most venturesome work was done on a small scale, and after 1894 many of his earlier small sculptures were enlarged by the excellent technician, Henri Lebossé.

Rodin's self-education included extensive reading in French literature, and he early knew the friendship and support of many of France's most important literary figures. Although he always remained a controversial artist, the critical literature was increasingly favourable from the 1880s onwards; so that by the time of his great one-man exhibition in 1900, his worldwide fame was solidly established. His clientele included royalty and millionaires, the most beautiful women in French and English society, politicians and artists. Rodin's productivity owed much to the many skilled professional sculptors who carved his marbles and enlarged or reduced his figures for bronze casting. This customary practice was well known to his patrons.

An ardent patriot who came to see his role as a great artist as important to the prestige of his country, Rodin accepted more major commissions than he could finish. He determined by 1900 to leave a museum of his art, and shortly before his death in 1917, he gave the state all his property, which included the great archive from which these photographs come, more than 7,000 drawings, and a sculpture collection so vast that there is still no complete inventory.

Rodin on photography

Rodin was the first artist to receive in his lifetime truly worldwide acclaim. Before his death on 17 November 1917, at the age of seventy-seven, he had enjoyed at least twenty years of homage from five continents, England and Japan, not merely as the finest living sculptor, but as the greatest artist of his time. Photography had been essential to the establishment of his reputation. In 1898, for example, he could exhibit his proposed monument to Balzac and know that in a matter of weeks it would be reproduced photographically in Tokyo, Hanoi, London, New York, Algiers, Berlin, Stockholm, Prague, Buenos Aires and Milwaukee.

> When I saw it reproduced in the Milwaukee newspaper, it seemed the most wonderful thing I had ever seen. It was not just a statue of a man, it was the very embodiment of a tribute to genius. It looked like a mountain come to life. It stirred up my interest in going to Paris, where artists of Rodin's stature lived and worked.

This is quoted from the autobiography of the photographer Edward Steichen, who became a major interpreter of Rodin's art and who himself knew worldwide fame.

It is ironic that an important way of rediscovering one of the most photographed sculptors in history should be through old photographs, proofs and documentary shots as well as artistic prints, often taken under Rodin's supervision in the studios and Salons. What sculptures have suffered more from photographic overexposure than *The Thinker* and *The Kiss*? But we can now experience them afresh, in the first moments of their completion, thanks to the Musée Rodin archives in Paris (Plates 19–24, 108–9). With all respect to the many fine photographers who have interpreted his work since 1917, none has surpassed the achievements of the best who worked directly for the artist. Many of these old prints are of extraordinary quality and should be reckoned beside those of Steichen as contributions to the history of interpretative photography. Rodin knew how to attract to his art and himself the finest talent and to inspire these gifted men and women to surpass themselves on his behalf.

Since his death, Rodin's extensive involvement with photography has been forgotten. With one notable exception, his few recorded pronouncements make it appear that he had a low estimate of photography as art and contrasted it unfavourably with painting and sculpture. When asked by Paul Gsell to compare the capacities of artists and photographers to treat motion, Rodin gave this often quoted reply:

> . . . it is the artist who is truthful and it is photography which lies, for in reality time does not stop, and if the artist succeeds in producing the impression of a movement which takes several moments for accomplishment, his work is certainly less conventional than the scientific image, where time is suspended.

Rodin was one of the original subscribers to Eadweard Muybridge's *Animal Locomotion*, which first appeared in 1887, and undoubtedly studied it closely. He disparaged documentary photography, because for him serious art required the artist to interpret his subjects and touch the viewer's emotions. Late in life, in what was titled 'My Testament', he offered the maxim, 'Mere exactitude, of which photography and moulage [life-casting] are the lowest forms, does not inspire feelings.' Much earlier, in a letter sent to the mayor of Calais in January 1889, he made these 'lowest forms' synonymous: 'Many cast from nature, that is to say, replace an art work with a photograph. It is quick but is not art.' Ironically, it is through these old photographs and new evidence in the Meudon Reserve that we can see how Rodin did in fact cast from cloth and paper when he needed to add drapery to a statue in progress, and photography helped him study the effect.

In a statement published in *Camera Work* in October 1908, Rodin showed under what circumstances he credited photography as serious art:

> I believe that photography can create works of art, but hitherto it has been extraordinarily bourgeois and babbling. No one ever suspected what could be got out of it; one doesn't even know today what one can expect from a process which permits of such profound sentiment, and such thorough interpretation of the model, as has been realized in the hands of Steichen. I consider Steichen a very great artist and the leading, the greatest photographer of the time. Before him nothing conclusive had been achieved. It is a matter of absolute indifference to me whether the photographer does, or does not, intervene. I do not know to what degree Steichen interprets, and I do not see any harm whatever, or of what importance it is, what means he uses to achieve his results. I care only for the result, which, however, must always remain clearly a photograph. It will always be interesting when it is the work of an artist.

Even photography's limitations, as he saw them, served Rodin, for they helped articulate what he wanted from sculpture. Comparing photography's capacity for exactitude with his own artistic intentions, he told Charles Chincholle in 1898 about his problems and doubts concerning his *Balzac*, 'For me modern sculpture cannot be photography. The artist must work not only with his hand but above all with his brain.' To Paul Gsell he observed:

> If the artist only reproduces superficial features as photography does, if he copies the lineaments of a face exactly, without reference to character, he deserves no admiration. The resemblance he ought to obtain is that of the soul . . . it is that which the sculptor . . . should seek beneath the mask of the features.

'Mere exactitude' served him well, however, as we recognize from the countless photographs of those who sat for him or had their posthumous portraits made by his hands, such as Balzac, Bastien Lepage and Barbey d'Aurevilly. Photographs of the dead helped him find likenesses among the living, and here, too, as we have recently discovered in the case of a man who resembled Balzac, he might have recourse to a photograph as well as to the actual model. Rodin's method did, in fact, presuppose a workmanlike reconnaissance of facial lineaments of the 'mask'. Photographs helped when sittings were limited. Only in the painfully won final stages did he turn to intuition and the agonies of imparting to the clay his model's spirit. In these moments photography with its 'frozen' expression was of no assistance, as he sought to make 'all the features expressive in the revelation of a conscience'.

Rodin's involvement with photography and his relations with photographers

Unlike Medardo Rosso and Brancusi, who personally photographed their sculpture as an aesthetic imperative, there is no evidence as yet that Rodin ever took a photograph. Nevertheless, his acquaintance with photography began early. As a youth, he sat before the lens of a childhood friend, Charles Aubry, who became a professional photographer. In 1863, he posed next to his bust of Father Eymard. This type of conventional or trophy-like photograph he caused to have taken all his life, but it does not reveal his sensibility to the medium. Missing from the great photographic collection in the Musée Rodin are contemporary photographs of the sculptures Rodin did from about 1863 until 1877, when, in order to make a living, he was working for employers in Paris and Belgium and permitted others to sign their name to his works. His partnership agreement with the Belgian sculptor Van Rasbourg, for example, specified that the latter would sign his name to all their works exhibited in Belgium, whereas Rodin would sign for their sculptures shown in other countries. In late 1876, or early 1877, he had a Brussels photographer named Marconi make straightforward documentary photographs of the plaster *Age of Bronze* (initially titled *The Vanquished*), his first publicly exhibited statue, which established his reputation as a statue-maker (Plates 2, 5). The photographs served both as a basis for a drawing and as a record for the artist.

When in the spring of 1877 a Paris Salon jury claimed that *The Vanquished* had been cast from life, Rodin wrote to Brussels at the jury's suggestion to ask the model, Auguste

Neyt, to go to a photographer and have himself photographed naked in the pose he had assumed for the sculpture. Along with an actual life cast made at his request, these photographs (Plates 3, 4) were the means by which the artist hoped for vindication. He was disappointed, as neither the photographs nor the life cast (which has not been found) seem to have been consulted by any juror other than the sculptor Falguière, who did look at the photographs. This traumatic incident and the use of photography to justify as well as explain his way of working may have determined Rodin to employ the medium in new ways for his profession.

In 1878, when working on *Saint John the Baptist Preaching*, Rodin had photographs taken of the plaster figure in the late stages of work (Plates 9–12). This later became his frequent practice, and the photographs served the same purpose as plaster casts or *estampages* (as he referred to impressions made of his work in progress), in that they recorded changing states of an evolving figure. A few years later he did the same thing with the Ugolino group while it was still in clay (Plates 27, 28), and in this instance the photograph may have encouraged him to make an important change in Ugolino's head. Rodin may have been the first sculptor to use photography to record and edit stages through which an important work had to pass during the clarification of his thought. Until he turned the enlargement of his figures over to Henri Lebossé in 1889 or the early 1890s, he did not mechanically increase their size from the model, but made important changes while at work on the final scale, changes that in some cases it now appears he wished to document. These alterations meant not just refining the clay surface, as we can now see in the marvellous documentary photographs of the life-size *Burghers of Calais* (Plates 51–9), but changing the positions of extremities.

In 1900, with the help of influential and wealthy friends, Rodin held what amounted to the first retrospective exhibition by a sculptor. He built a pavilion near the Pont d'Alma in Paris, opposite the gates to the great World Fair of that year on the Champ de Mars. Just inside the entrance to the pavilion there was a small gallery in which seventy-one photographs taken by Eugène Druet were exhibited and sold by the photographer, who was allowed to keep all the proceeds. Druet, whose Café du Yacht Club Français was just across the street, was also the manager of the exhibition until he and Rodin had a disagreement. After 1900, there were frequent exhibitions of photographs of Rodin's work. Following a reconciliation with Druet, for example, the latter showed several photographs at the Galerie des Artistes Modernes in May 1901. There was great demand for their exhibition throughout Europe, particularly in Germany.

By the mid-1890s, photographers such as Giraudon and Pol Marsan were applying for permission to photograph the artist and his work, and thereafter they competed with each other on contracts and assignments. Rodin seems to have encouraged the photographers he met professionally or socially to come to his studio. That it was he who encouraged Druet to become a photographer is denied by Laurent Vizzavona, whose father worked for the sculptor and was a rival photographer. Druet, who invented a camera that could take panoramic pictures, worked for Rodin from 1896 on. Rodin sat for the finest portrait photographers of his age, such as Braun, Nadar, Steichen, Kasebier and Coburn. The Musée Rodin archives have a marvellous collection of these portraits. Requests for reproductions of his work from the press, publishers, artists and admirers began to increase after the 1889 exhibition which Rodin held with Claude Monet at the Galerie Georges Petit. As more of his works entered museums not only in France but throughout the world, this demand accelerated. (Bulloz complained to Rodin that the negative of the marble *Eternal Spring* had worn out and had to be replaced.) By 1900, these demands had reached staggering proportions and came to include requests for pictures of work in progress from committees which had commissioned monuments such as those for Puvis de Chavannes and Whistler.

From correspondence and business contracts between Rodin and the photographers Druet, Bulloz, Haweis and Coles, we can begin to reconstruct his relationship with these men, and with respect to the first two, the part he played in the taking of the photographs. At least by the 1890s it became his practice to insist upon seeing and approving all proofs taken by those who worked in his studios. This is why the Musée Rodin archives are so rich in first and second states. He often gave detailed and precise instructions verbally to the professional photographers, or himself edited the proofs with a wash or by pencil markings (see, eg, Plates 83, 86, 87). His standards were exacting, and he was a difficult man to please. A note from Druet in the file in the Musée Rodin indicates he had destroyed plates rejected by the artist. Several such notes confirm that the photographers had diligently carried out the requested revisions. In 1898, Pol Marsan wrote that he would bring proofs and that he had scrupulously followed the sculptor's prescriptions. Adolphe Braun assured Rodin that his photos had been carefully done and worked up just for him. In his contract of 1900 with Druet, Rodin reserved the right to cancel any photographs that he deemed 'insufficiently artistic'. In the 1903 agreement with Bulloz, pertaining to an album of 103 photographs for which Rodin was to pay the expenses, the sculptor insisted that the pictures should not be sold separately, that their size should be determined by the sculpture's importance, and, upon the advice of his lawyer, E. Valtuer, he reserved the right of the 'artistic direction of the photography relative to their lighting and disposition'. Unquestionably, Rodin did often collaborate with some of his best photographers. On 6 January 1901, in a touching letter meant to repair the rupture between them, Druet recounted to Rodin something of the history of their relationship: 'Ever since I have known you and you asked me to photograph your works, I have been amenable to all your requirements, I accepted your advice and your direction and I scrupulously conformed to your wishes.'

Although he may not have been the first artist to do so, Rodin had his signature affixed by means of a transparent 'maquette' to the plates signed by Druet. (Courbet, for one, signed his name on the prints taken from his paintings by Victor Laisné.) It is probable that Rodin came to look upon his most frequently used photographers such as Druet and Bulloz as being *practiciens*, like the highly skilled professional sculptors who assisted in the studio. This was not the case with the young American Edward Steichen, to whom, even before he saw the proofs, Rodin gave 2,000 francs for photographing the *Balzac* at night (Plate 117). 'A fabulous gift for one night's work,' exclaimed the photographer in his 1963 autobiography. (Rodin's ablest *practiciens* averaged about one franc an hour or roughly sixty francs a week.) In daylight Steichen had found the plaster to have a 'harsh chalky effect', and it was Rodin who then suggested that he photograph it by moonlight. (In an article for *Art in America* written in 1969, Steichen seems to have forgotten that the project was Rodin's idea and claimed it for his own.) Steichen wrote in his autobiography, 'I agreed with Rodin. . . . I had no guide to refer to, and I had to guess at the exposure. I spent the whole night photographing the Balzac. I gave varying exposures from fifteen minutes to an hour.' Further to express his appreciation, Rodin also gave Steichen three bronze sculptures, one of which was a cast of the small version of *The Walking Man* that 'was to be a symbol for me of what he hoped my whole life would be – a continuous marching onward'.

By 1900, Rodin had evolved a considerable system for the production and sale of his work. An astute businessman, he preferred not to tie himself to art dealers, although willing to sell them work. His photographers often negotiated sales of sculptures and sent him visitors. Steichen did much to increase Rodin's reputation in America through exhibitions of the artist's work. Rodin saw to it that he got handsome royalties on the photographs, and Bulloz contracted to give him 200 francs a year. Many admirers and clients found their way to Rodin's studios from Bulloz's shop in the Rue Bonaparte. No matter where his sculptures were exhibited after 1900, he would not let them be photographed without his consent. Bulloz was his watchdog to see that unauthorized photographs were not reproduced.

Rodin's business relations with photographers were not always satisfactory to them. Some, such as Adolphe Braun, found the terms of contracts unacceptable, or, in the case of the young Americans Haweis and Coles, impossible to live with. Their prints would not sell at the ten francs necessary to pay Rodin's royalty and still make a profit. Further, they had to sell them through Bulloz, who charged one and a half francs for putting Rodin's stamp on them. Rodin did reduce his demands. Druet cited the indignity of having to sell his work through a competitor, Giraudon, whose shop was (and still is) near the École des Beaux-Arts, because Rodin wanted to be sure that the students at the École and in that quarter would see his art. Photographers found it a hardship to give the master unlimited free prints, and the older, more established ones, like Braun, arranged a reduced price. Druet claimed the right to copyright his prints, which seems to have offset giving the sculptor prints without charge.

The range and quality of more than a thousand photographs in the Musée Rodin archives strongly suggest that the artist valued photographers for more than their help in meeting commercial demands. He also recognized the interpretative as well as the technical skills of the 'operators' who hauled their heavy and cumbersome view cameras, tripods and glass plates to the various Paris studios and by boat and carriage to Meudon when weather and light permitted. It is customary to think that only Edward Steichen produced imaginative or artistic photographs of the artist and his work, but this is unjust to men like Eugène Druet, Charles Bodmer, D. Freuler, Vizzavona, J.-E. Bulloz, Stephen Haweis, Henry W. Coles and others. Many seem to have found contact with the great artist intellectually exhilarating and important to their own development. For young artists Rodin was a model of audacity based on craft, patience, self-discipline and decisiveness about art. All seemed to take pride in contributing to his renown and in outdoing one another in the interpretation of his intentions.

It was demands for pictures from artists as well as journalists, authors and patrons that caused photographers to recognize that their fame and possibly fortune could be ensured by working with Rodin. Haweis and Coles endured a harsh contract for a time in the hope of these rewards. Druet's becoming an art dealer in 1903 may have been helped by his association with the world's greatest living artist. Rodin, in turn, may have been one of the first sculptors to have benefited from the modern slide lecture. Between 1900 and 1914, Bulloz supplied lecturers such as Rilke, V. Pica and M. Gasperi with slides for their speaking tours. In 1899, Arthur J. Eddy, whose portrait had been done by Rodin, lectured on his work at the Chicago Art Institute, using photographs supplied by the artist and projected with a stereopticon.

Photography as a stage in the evolution of a sculpture, and sculpture staged for photography

To understand how Rodin on occasion used photography to create rather than document a sculpture, it helps to know how he worked. One of the traits of this Promethean artist was economy of means. Starting in the late 1870s, there were many times, for example, when photographs served him as a convenient basis for making drypoint prints as well as drawings with which to illustrate his sculpture in salon catalogues. (Dr Kirk Varnedoe will show this source of Rodin prints and drawings in a forthcoming essay.) The grid pencilled over the early photograph of *John the Baptist* (Plate 10) guided Rodin in the making of a drawing. A dark photograph of the final plaster of *Balzac* (not here reproduced) has stylus marks that relate it to a separate sketch or transfer the artist made.

Photographs as well as contemporary commentaries remind us of Rodin's practice of marking his marbles with graphite where he wanted or foresaw changes (Plate 41). He both exhibited and sold carved stones so marked. (Much to his annoyance, one client tried to erase the graphite markings on a marble and complained in a letter to Rodin about the resulting smudge.) Few even in the artist's lifetime understood that when he sold a marble, he did not necessarily consider it finished or unalterable, unless it was a replica. For Rodin, art was a continuum, uninterrupted by its realization in permanent form or disposal by sale. Rather than searching for perfection and conclusions, Rodin looked upon all that he did as potential beginnings for new variations or new outcomes. The notion that because of lack of formal training and self-discipline Rodin was incapable of finishing a work is contradicted by the fact that for half of his creative life he produced sculpture that was finished by conventional standards.

Rodin took pleasure in his skill and in doing things well. By nature, however, he was a compulsive editor and an artist who always wanted to keep his options open. What drove him was the conviction that he could always do things differently, if not better, and that he must push himself and his art further, not towards perfection, but into unknown territory. This voyage of discovery did not depend so much on skill as on artistic intuition and the ability to improvise in modelling while ignoring finesse. He habitually set sculptures aside before completion and would seem to ignore them for long periods of time. He would then look at them afresh, using photographs as well, as if in rediscovery. Photographs of the studio show works on the floor, in corners, on top of cupboards and over doorways – sculpture-in-waiting, so to speak, or, as Rilke aptly called it, sculpture in a state of growth. Photographs gave him another form of critical detachment, for even in the small selection here published we now see that with pen or pencil he would frequently indulge himself in what he could do or might have done. These photographs remind us that Rodin tied his art to processes of thought rather than to preconceptions.

Consider the types of graphic editing here sampled. The first might be called augmenting the characterization of a subject, as when he changed the hair styles of *Claude Lorrain* and *Victor Hugo* (Plates 75, 87) or cancelled out the clay cranial formations of *The Thinker* and *Ugolino* (Plates 19, 27). The most startling interpretative drawing over a photograph is that done on *Eustache de St Pierre* (Plate 51), where Rodin penned the shadows that furrow face and shroud. He may have been showing the photographer how he desired greater contrast in the final print. Eustache was, however, the crucial figure in the commission for *The Burghers of Calais* and the one about which Rodin worried the most. The Calais City Council had originally sought a single statue not only to commemorate the fourteenth-century heroes, but also to vindicate Eustache, their leader, from the charge, lodged by Voltaire, of having been a traitor who advocated surrender of the beseiged city in order to benefit from the gratitude of the English king. Rodin knew that of all the burghers, Eustache would receive the most critical attention from his commissioners. (He in fact exhibited the figure separately.) Compositionally, the old warrior was critical for initiating the six-act drama. The sculpture thus carried a heavy political and artistic burden that caused Rodin repeatedly to rethink its details, from the positioning of its fingers and feet to the depths of the shadows. The figure of Eustache was photographed more than that of any other burgher.

Along with enhancing a sculpture's expressiveness, Rodin's editing was directed towards greater compositional clarity and unity. One of his least-known but major works is *Christ and Mary Magdalene*, which, though never publicly exhibited, was carved twice in marble for clients. In what may be the most audacious interpretation of the relation of Mary to Christ in art history, Rodin's startling and brilliant plaster still remains apart from public view in the reserves of the Rodin Museum in Meudon. Rodin was dissatisfied with the positioning of Mary's right leg in a marble version and redrew it on a print in order to strengthen her stance and to clarify that part of the composition (Plate 103). Too often has Rodin been charged with being a composer of details and not totalities, but, as seen in several of his editings, he was mindful of the total effect. He also pondered the relation of his statues to their supports and worried with his pen over the profiles of the bases and pedestals, visible in reworkings for the monuments to Claude Lorrain and Victor Hugo, and in *The Walking Man* (Plates 73, 86, 132). One of the more drastic examples of reconceiving the rapport of sculpture with its support took the form of drawing a whole new curved background upon the tipped flat plaster base of *The Metamorphoses of Ovid* (Plate 77). The ink shapes drawn on the lower section of '*I Am Beautiful*' (Plate 30) may have been in anticipation of its being carved in stone and were possibly intended as a guide to a *practicien*. Rodin appears to have felt the need to counterbalance the swelling mass at the top of the sculpture, indicating that more stone should be left at the base of a future carving. This striving for greater unity extended to reworking even a single figure, the enlarged and final version of the monument to Balzac. According to the French artist Stanislas Lami, who knew Rodin's assistants and wrote on his work, it was not possible for Rodin to make alterations in Lebossé's enlargements. He could incise or carve the plaster,

Plaster hand hanging from a cord. Date unknown.
Photo Freuler, salt print, 11.5 × 7.9 cm (cat. no. 1334)

however. On a photograph of the final plaster of *Balzac* he drew a line to extend the furrows of the hair and collar into the lapel of the robe (Plate 113). In that same picture there is visible his drawing on the actual plaster neck that he was to criticize to others as being too large.

Rodin's process of testing a sculpture continually to find new ways to achieve a different expressiveness was both recorded and abetted by photographs. In the former case photographers documented his essays in reorientating sculptures from their original relation to the ground. (We have to distinguish such experiments from the practical requirements of tilting a sculpture upward in order to get more natural light to facilitate the photography, as with a picture of *Fugitive Love*, Plate 32.) Rodin experimented with showing the *Hand of God* in marble as a relief, balanced on a corner of its base and tilted upward (Plates 105, 106). Each shift of position affects the implications of the theme. A small photograph shows how he hung a plaster hand by a string from a hook to ponder its response to gravity. (This particular study may have been made in connection with *The Burghers of Calais*.) On two prints of the marble or plaster *Young Girl Kissed by a Phantom* (Plates 81, 82), the artist made notations to change a pose and to indicate where deeper cutting, shadows, or perhaps wings might be introduced, but he also reconceived the horizontal composition in terms of two upright caryatids. This last is a reminder of his lifetime of doing architectural decoration.

Photography occasionally inspired Rodin to compose or stage situations with his figures. We cannot be sure that the two couples seen in Plates 135 and 136 survived the photographing. There is some doubt whether the proposed monument to Puvis de

Bust of *Victor Hugo* facing two plaster casts of
Meditation. Plaster, date unknown. Photo Haweis and
Coles?, gelatin silver print, 23.3 × 16.8 cm (cat. no. 1360)

Chavannes (Plate 125), which shows the bust, a table, a plaster cast of an apple tree and the
Spirit of Eternal Repose, was assembled just for the camera, but there seems no question
that this was the motive for bringing together two casts of *The Tragic Muse* or *Meditation* to
confront the bust of Victor Hugo like devotees at a shrine. From old photographs we gain
an idea of how the artist spent a good part of his life, not working directly from the live
model, but as a dramatist always in search of new encounters for his vast repertory of
plaster performers. How much Rodin cared about the *mise-en-scène* of his 'museums', as
the studios were known after 1900, we know both from photographs and from the
abundant transport bills that detail how many men had to move big sculptures not only
among but also within the ateliers.

Demystifying the studio and the making of sculpture

Between the late 1890s and 1917, there was probably no artist's studio visited by more
people than Rodin's. His ateliers early won the reputation of being wonders to experience.
The Musée Rodin files are stuffed with telegrams, *cartes bleues* and letters from people all
over the world requesting visits. Judging by the countless letters of appreciation, most
seem to have succeeded. Even before 1890, a visit to Rodin's studio became highly
desirable for artists, critics, writers and government officials concerned with the arts.
Thereafter, for international society and royalty a trip to Paris had to include a visit to see
the great artist. On certain days he opened his studios in the Dépôt des Marbres and at
Meudon to receive visitors. In 1900 and after it was moved to Meudon, Rodin's pavilion

for his exhibition at the Pont d'Alma came to be known as 'Le Musée Rodin'. This may explain why on 24 January 1911, Karl Baedeker wrote to the mayor of Meudon asking what were the hours of the 'Musée Rodin'. When Rodin himself replied that his studios were not open to the public, Baedeker immodestly answered that he understood Rodin's reasons full well, for 'the consequences of a mention in my guide would have been a terrible inconvenience' to the artist.

Receiving many visitors was customary among successful artists. In Rodin's case, however, it might be added that he came to see it as his duty to receive the world just as it had become his obligation to be its greatest artist. He also preferred to sell directly out of his studio. He enjoyed educating into his art everyone who was interested. Today the studios are gone, but visiting Rodin's former home at the Hôtel Biron in Paris is a welcome substitute, so intended by the artist. Looking at the old photographs, one can make a kind of studio tour and have the feeling that the artist had this in mind when he had so many views taken showing clusters of sculptures and works in progress.

Unlike some of his affluent contemporaries in sculpture and painting, Rodin did not furnish his studios with the trophies of financial success. One painting, a copy of Rembrandt's *Bathsheba*, now in the Musée Rodin, hung on a studio wall, a photograph of Raphael's *Disputa* could be seen in the studio where the *Burghers* were made (Plates 50, 51), and there was a portrait print of Bastien-Lepage (visible in Plate 38). Otherwise, photographs of the studios confirm the description by Edmond de Goncourt on 17 March 1886 of their austere ambience:

> I found him in his studio on the Boulevard Vaugirard, the ordinary atelier of the sculptor, with the walls splashed with plaster, his miserable cast-iron stove, the cold humidity coming from all the great 'machines' of wet clay, which were wrapped in rags, and with all his casts of heads, arms and legs.

Rilke wrote in 1903:

> Rodin had several studios, some that are well known, in which visitors and letters found him. There were others in out-of-the-way, secluded places of which no one knew. These rooms were like cells, bare, poor and grey with dust, but their poverty was like the great grey poverty of God out of which trees bud in March.

Just as he would turn a clay figure on its revolving stand for de Goncourt and Bracquemond, Rodin had his photographers shoot his *Burghers* turned on their 'saddles' to show their changing aspect (Plates 55, 56). What is missing from visitors' accounts is the usual quiet and simple eloquence of the artist's response to questions and his honest joy at the involvement and enthusiasm of a visitor such as Malvina Hoffman, who reported what it was like to be left alone with the sculptures for an hour or so. A guest's solitary communion with his plasters he felt was sufficient. Then there were times when the older and much-decorated Rodin, attired by a London bespoke tailor, hosted government delegations and pontificated.

Rodin's opening of his ateliers to visitors and photographers may well have been intended to counter the popular mystique of an artist's studio and to foster understanding of the work and skill that the making of art involved. Rodin viewed himself as an artist who

Rodin discussing his ideas, 1911. Photo Manuel, gelatin silver print, 15.4 × 22.5 cm (cat. no. 1338)

was a skilled worker rather than a magician. He wanted the world after his death to focus attention upon his works, even those *en chemin* or rejected for sale and exhibition. He did want his cancelled stone sculptures to be seen in the Hôtel Biron, which was unusual for a sculptor. Just as unusual and surprising was what he chose to show the world on postcards as well as in published photographs. It is hard to imagine any sculptor today, no matter how famous, having postcards made bearing pictures of his work in progress rather than finished. Rodin did this in connection with his reworked plaster relief of *La France*, which circulated round the world. J. E. Bulloz made beautiful prints of several views of the bust of Antonin Proust, still in what appears to be clay and possessed of its armature, which projected mast-like from the top of the head (Plate 46). Clearly visible are the plaster-covered wood or metal struts in the bust area, possibly built up preliminary to broadening the work. According to Judith Cladel and Malvina Hoffman, it was Rodin's practice to press clay into plaster piece moulds taken from a portrait he was working on so that he could keep the original and make changes in the new clay impression. This photograph and that of the plaster mask of Rose Beuret (Plate 16), the artist's lifelong mistress, show his frequent acceptance of casting seams left by the moulds, perhaps partly because they constituted a kind of accidental drawing that calls our attention to surface modulations in surprising ways. This would be particularly apt in plasters, where nuance can be obscured

Postcard of *La France*. Plaster and clay, date unknown.
Photo Bulloz (cat. no. 1336)

Postcard of *The Little Shade*. Bronze, before 1902.
Photographer unknown (cat. no. 1364). The card was
printed in Japan and addressed to Rodin by a Japanese
artist, postmark 1902.

and light absorbed. Rodin's custom of adding clay to plaster busts in order to rework them
is documented in the photographs of the bust of Barbey d'Aurevilly by a photographer
from the *World's Graphic Press* (Plates 123, 124). In the Meudon Reserve there are still
some plasters with clay additions, notably the *Clemenceau* studies, that will some day be on
public view.

Starting with the Marconi photograph of the back of the plaster *Age of Bronze* (Plate 5),
in which there is clearly visible a metal pin that holds the left arm to the shoulder, Rodin
publicized the studio mechanics of joining his forms. In a marvellous conjunction, a
photographer showed the bandaged clay figures of *Eustache de St Pierre* as if looking away
from a maquette for a monument to the Argentine statesman, Vicuña-McKenna (Plate
72). Rodin's struggle to adjust the wrists and feet to just the right angle caused the
wrapping of the extremities. We know from the American sculptor Malvina Hoffman, who
studied with Rodin, that he would have assistants cut off limbs of plaster figures and that
he would then replace them with new ones, using white wax as an adhesive. The reproduced photograph of the plaster version of *The Crouching Woman* (Plate 96) shows his

assemblage of a figure from disparate sources, including the head of *Iris*. The joining has been done by the white wax Hoffman described. Rodin obviously approved this photograph, for Druet made prints of it to be sold to the public.

Like many of the artists of his generation, Rodin translated his figures into different media, at times letting a patron determine whether it would be in bronze or marble. In what appears to have been an untypical gesture, Rodin had the camera record on occasion the progress of this translation. We can see, therefore, a cast of *The Martyr* propped up on a vertical armature to serve as the model for a *metteur au point*, then the same form roughed out in stone, and finally the last state as finished by a *practicien* (Plates 40–2). The photographs showing the plaster and marble figures of *Orpheus and Eurydice Leaving Hell* (Plates 101, 102) give us a good idea of how the carvers would change and make more consistent in modelling works that were hybrid in origin. There was never any secret or uncertainty about the fact that Rodin employed skilled professional sculptors such as Bourdelle, Despiau, Escoula, Peter and others to carve his work. Clients would, in fact, sometimes ask for a certain *practicien*. That Rodin had himself photographed carving was also to remind the public of his participation as well as supervision of the stone sculptures.

No artist before him seems to have exercised the opportunity of sharing with the public his pleasure in the work of art, the prosaic yet fascinating stages through which a form could emerge. Among his many gifts, Rodin was a teacher, and throughout his life, in conversations with writers, his own writings, and in photography, the public were considered his students. As a great teacher, he freely shared the discovery of the effects achievable by chance and accident. How he would complete a sculpture by its unmaking can be seen in the photograph of *Meditation* (Plate 38). In this and other partial figures, consider the contrasts he proposed: the most lifelike sculpture seen in conjunction with the undisguised mechanics of its making and unmaking, illusion married to anti–illusion, and the natural with artifice. Photography helped accustom the world to Rodin's frequent practice of employing various modes within a single work or within couples or groups of figures (Plates 37, 39), in daring opposition to the tradition of making a sculpture in a single style. Over a number of years he developed a new concept of completeness in sculpture as an alternative to traditional norms of finish. This meant that he would arrest a work when to go further would detract from the effect he had arrived at by hard work and intuition – an effect he could not have foreseen. A head or arm might be left undefined, hands unmodelled or even detached, or the scale of two figures out of proportion to each other. It must have required self-discipline and provided a certain satisfaction for him to withhold his skill from his creations under particular circumstances. This last outraged some critics and members of the public who felt cheated of seeing whole figures. In sum, Rodin loved his *métier* and sharing all that made possible what for him was the triumph of art.

How to see and photograph sculpture

Looking at nineteenth-century photographs of the sculpture made by Rodin's contemporaries such as Falguière and Bartholomé, whose work is well represented in the Musée Rodin photographic collection, one is struck by the fact that they are nearly all fully-lighted frontal views so that the work's subject, details and workmanship are clearly visible. There are only occasional side and rarely back views, suggesting that the photographers emulated the few basic angles from which the sculptor worked. As he did with the studio assistants who modelled, carved, and enlarged or reduced his works, Rodin educated the photographers into his way of seeing by insisting on personal direction of their work. Repeatedly, photographers note when sending prints that they have succeeded in 'understanding' him.

The first lesson with a new photographer must have been Rodin's own most important revelation when he was learning his *métier* as a modeller: to see forms in depth and not in the plane. 'Always consider a surface as the extremity of a volume, as if it were a smaller or larger point turned in your direction.' This view was shared with many earlier sculptors such as Cellini, but Rodin claimed it was taught to him during his apprenticeship by an older decorative sculptor named Constant Simon. (It was one of Rodin's virtues to credit his sources.) For the most part, but not entirely, Rodin's photographers followed his injunction not to freeze the sculptures frontally or treat them as reliefs. We thus see his sculptures in terms of their thickness and not just their breadth. Uninhibited by the motif's unintelligibility, some photographers took daring foreshortened views, such as that by Bulloz of *Ariadne* exhibited in the 1905 Salon, in which we see only the backs of the legs (Plate 127). Druet took a head-on view of *Despair*, so that the woman's raised foot points directly at us (Plate 93). Photographing *The Helmet-Maker's Wife* (Plate 50), Druet got so close and went so far under the figure that the nearest portion is out of focus. Rodin approved this distortion, which evokes optical distortions of things seen close up, by signing the negative.

Druet is supposed to have introduced Rodin to the artificial lighting of sculpture. With the exception of some photographs Druet took using a magnesium loop and reflectors, Rodin preferred his 'operators' to use the same single source of light that he himself employed in modelling and carving. Some of the most beautiful photographs, such as that of the torso of *The Martyr* (Plate 44), were back-lighted. When the form is shown against the light, as was often done by Haweis and Coles, we are made fully aware of the expressive contours and the drawing action of light (Plates 25, 26). Druet's series of the bronze *Eve*, taken as the light faded in the studio at the Dépôt des Marbres, recalls Rodin's discussions of critically analysing his sculpture by studying the big planes and their interrelation when the sun was setting outside the studio. Under these circumstances, the diminishing light masked small details and threw into greater prominence both the silhouette and the major areas of modelling. Not surprisingly, then, Rodin enjoined his photographers to work with shadows. Druet and others were thus encouraged to cloak in darkness such figures as *Eve* and *The Kneeling Faun* (Plates 97, 98). Although it was customary practice for photographers of the Photo-Secession, we have no evidence that other sculptors of the time ever considered having their works photographed at twilight or by moonlight.

Of all Rodin's sculptures, those in marble benefited most from sensitive employment of darkness. (He enjoyed showing his works in stone by candlelight, though he was not the first to do so.) If one looks at hundreds of nineteenth-century documentary shots of marble sculptures, it is a joy to encounter the prints of *The Head of Sorrow* and *Eve Fairfax* (Plates

121, 122). Bulloz makes us realize today why Rodin's art in stone was not only universally desired but coveted more than his bronzes in the artist's lifetime. Imaginatively photographed, the white marble heads could be made to seem more human than when actually confronted. Rodin knew how marble could arrogate light to itself and with its blond shadows glow in a Victorian interior. So wrote his clients, particularly those in England, when describing their pleasure at contemplating his radiant stones in their homes.

Photography permitted Rodin to teach the world his egalitarian views on the expressiveness of the human body. Rare would be the sculptor since his time who would have postcards made showing just the back of a standing figure. Such a postcard of a small sculpture called *The Little Shade* was printed in Japan and circulated by 1902. Some of the artist's sculptures are known to us only by photographs taken from the back or sides. Among the oldest photographs are those of the back view of the *Seated Ugolino* (Plate 6), modelled before 1877 and photographed around 1880. Among the most striking is that of the back view of *The Shade* (Plate 36), standing out-of-doors next to the studio. The model had been a Paris strong man, and Rodin had been taken with the power and beauty of his back. No doubt Rodin admired Steichen's photography and the several beautiful prints of naked models seen from the back that were shown to him when the photographer sought access to the master and his studios in 1902. Steichen recalls in his autobiography that the models were shy of the camera and preferred being photographed from the rear.

The camera helped the public adjust to Rodin's insights into the formal completeness and varied life of his figural parts and partial figures (a figural part being a hand or foot, for example, while a partial figure is a torso without some or all of the rest of the parts of the body). The dramatic sequence of Druet's prints of the *Clenched Hand* (Plates 65–70), framed by a blanket and seen from different viewpoints, gave the public an understanding of why he often did not permanently attach a small sculpture to a base. What Rodin was telling us through these pictures is that we do not know his work until we have seen it in all of its possible orientations. When pondering these prints, it is as if Rodin is looking over our shoulder and pointing out how a hand can become an animal or reptile crawling up a hill or, crablike, walking across a beach. The same gesture rotated can be made to implore, menace or recoil. Rodin cropped his figure of *Despair* with a blanket so that her headless form appears as if in a cave (Plate 94). (This was perhaps inspired by drawings he made around 1886 to accompany the text of Baudelaire's *Fleurs du Mal*, in which figures are sometimes seen in caves.) In the Meudon Reserve there are numerous plaster versions of *Despair* in which different limbs or the head itself is missing. As he did so often when alone in the studio or for the camera, Rodin posed an important question of early modern sculpture: what can sculpture do without?

From comments he made to reporters and friends, we know that with major public sculptures such as *The Burghers of Calais* and the *Balzac*, Rodin did not claim that they were equally successful from all points of view. He believed that these monuments succeeded compositionally from five or six angles. Given Rodin's collaboration with his photographers, these old photographs go far in answering the question from which points of view and from what distances they should be seen. The way the great gum-bichromate series surrounds *The Burghers* (Plates 60–4), for example, shows us how Rodin wanted us to circle the group (counter-clockwise, I would argue). The great distortions in *Balzac's* face make artistic and dramatic sense when the figure is seen from a distance of about twenty-five feet rather than from directly below, as it would seem Rodin's critics were wont to do. These exaggerations embody his idea of a modern monument and defy light and distance, which would have eaten into the planes and destroyed the detail of a finely finished, more usual treatment of the face. The recent contention of a famous American minimalist sculptor that the *Balzac* lacks a satisfying *Gestalt* from any angle would have surprised Steichen, Druet and Bulloz, particularly after they had photographed it from the front, back and sides in twilight and at night. These brilliant photographs, which throw the figure into silhouette (Plates 114–17), share with us Rodin's discovery of what he called his 'great lines'.

What did photographers teach Rodin?

If photography had not been invented before his death, there is no reason to believe that Rodin's sculpture would have been significantly changed. Photographs did aid, if not inspire, several drawings. The impact of his vision on photographers is more tangible than the reverse. It has been argued that Muybridge's studies of hands may have encouraged Rodin's conception of the partial figure as a complete work of art. We know from recent finds in the Meudon Reserve and from previous knowledge that Rodin had been making partial figures in the 1870s. Muybridge's photographs of parts of the body in motion were indeed like Rodin's *études* of figural parts, but the photographer did not build an art on his discovery, as did Rodin and later photographers.

Rodin is not on record, so far as we know, as having credited photographers with giving him new ideas, nor do we have written evidence of his having an aesthetic of the print. It is the Musée Rodin collection of photographs that argues for his appreciation of photography. Rodin must have observed and enjoyed the affinities between the medium of photography and his sculpture in terms of capturing light and its effects. He did not take sides in the contemporary controversies over whether or not photography should look like art. He seems to have been sympathetic to a wide variety of approaches. Photography taught him to look at his own works in a detached way and to experience unforeseeable but hoped-for effects. Photographers undoubtedly surprised him with their interpretations of his work, notably in the gum-bichromate prints that are so numerous in his collection of photographs (see Plates 24, 35, 60–4). This type of printing was popular in the 1890s and at the turn of the century as a way of emulating the effects of lithography and painting, thereby giving the photograph a more artistic look. To understand the process by which the photographs of the *Fallen Caryatid*, *The Thinker* and *The Burghers of Calais* were made, it is helpful to read in Steichen's *A Life in Photography* his discovery of the process before 1900:

> In one of the photographic magazines, I had read an article by Robert Demachy, a famous French photographer, about a process that he used extensively and referred to as a gum-bichromate process. This was a pigment process similar to the well-known carbon process, but he coated the paper himself. It appealed to me for two reasons. One was economy, and the other was the unusual quality that could be produced, unlike

anything printed on silver or platinum paper. The ingredients used in coating the paper were simply watercolour, in black, brown, or almost any other shade, and gum arabic. The sensitizing agent was bichromate of potash. The mixture was applied to paper with a brush as evenly as possible. When dry it became light sensitive. When it was placed under a negative and exposed to light, the action of the light hardened the pigment under the thin open parts of the negative, making it insoluble. The paper was developed by floating it on cold, warm or even hot water. Sometimes it took friction with a brush to remove the parts that were affected less by light. If the mixture was applied thick, the results were very granular, an excellent effect for some pictures representing broad masses of light and dark. When a thin coating was applied, it gave finer gradation and less grain. The paper was inexpensive to produce, and gave greater control of the final results than any other process.

In thick gum-bichromate prints not only are details often lost, but so are the contours, indispensable to Rodin's method of building a figure. Without these continuous peripheries, the figure fuses with the environment. When Rodin was meditating on *The Burghers of Calais*, he knew they would be seen in all lights and weathers, as they were to be situated out-of-doors. Since gum prints appear in France after 1894, those of *The Burghers* were probably taken either of the cast destined for Calais in 1895, or of one made in Belgium around 1904. These gum-bichromate prints gave Rodin a dramatic equivalent of the *Burghers'* appearance under a morning or twilight mist, the martyrs enveloped by atmosphere. Those of the *Fallen Caryatid* and *The Thinker* plotted for him his success in achieving the major planes and their disposition. While these prints did not show how the planes fitted together, they did register the broad relationships between the spottings of highlights and shadows, which for Rodin were critical in achieving a successful overall effect. Further, the details not reproduced in this type of print included the sculpture's texture and relation to its base, so that its material, bronze or plaster, would be in doubt, but not the human presence. Today we may admire these gum prints as abstractions, and Rodin was probably aware of this aspect, but for him formal interest by itself was not enough for art. Gum printing entailed accidents, and there was no way to predict the print's precise final appearance. Rodin was the perfect courtier of accidents in his own work and he must have felt a kinship with his photographers in this regard. Sometimes he rationalized accidents and left them if they augmented the impression of a movement. This they certainly did in the gum series of *The Burghers*. Rodin's appreciation of this type of print was manifest in its use on posters announcing the exhibition of *The Thinker* in Strasbourg in 1905.

On seeing Rodin's art in the context of his studios

It is fair to ask what these photographs showing works in the studios and salons contribute to our understanding of Rodin that more recent pictures of isolated works do not? Taken, quite literally, from the artist's viewpoint, they show us the light and space in which Rodin's sculptures were made and judged. Paintings do not benefit from being photographed in studio surroundings. Looking at the great photographs made of *The Kiss* in

Rodin's atelier on the other hand (Plates 108, 109), one can forget how the mass media have made it a cliché. These beautifully composed pictures remind us of how Rodin's sculpture lives in light and belongs to both art and life.

The old pictures are often precious evidence of work now lost either because, as with the Vicuña-McKenna project (Plate 72), a commission was aborted, or because the artist decided before bronze-casting to subtract some portion of a composition, as with *Orpheus Imploring the Gods* (Plate 100). There were many works that never left the studios for exhibition and were not available to photographers after the artist's death. They included assembled figures or inspired impermanent couplings, for instance *The Tragic Muse* and *Son of Ugolino* (Plate 92), which were photographed for further study, but were then destroyed or perhaps dispersed either by the artist or those who cared for his estate but did not know his intentions. As examples, two of the most remarkable and poetic photographs ever taken of Rodin's art are by an as yet unidentified photographer (Plates 135, 136). They show pairs of small figures, one reclining in a basin, the other lacking a base but shown upright against a backdrop. Although only a few inches high, the figures have been photographed in an inspired way, as if in a moonlit world of their own. Since they are not framed in the exact centre of the print, one has the impression they cling together within a deep well of space. (The upright figures do in fact lean against each other for support.) The photographs capture and enhance that quality of Rodin's sculpture that prompted Rilke to write, 'Thoughts glide over it like shadows: new meanings arise like riddles and unfold into clear significance.'

Old prints that conjoin two or more sculptures in process, like *The Gates of Hell* and *Eternal Spring* (Plate 48), *Faun and Satyr* and a *Burgher of Calais* (Plate 71), bring home the simultaneity of his creative efforts that account for a productivity which many today still find hard to believe. In 1907, Rilke wrote:

> Now he begins one thing, completes another, modifies another, as if responding to their calls he passes through their midst and sees their need of him. He forgets none of them, those in the background bide their time and are in no hurry.

Even when at work on such exacting commissions as *The Burghers* and the monuments to Hugo and Balzac, Rodin would find relaxation and satisfaction in smaller conceptions that could be more promptly realized. The laborious work of enlarging his models could largely be left to assistants. Had not Rodin spent may years of his life before 1882 doing the work of others during the daytime and then modelling for himself at night and at weekends, alternating between styles demanded by employers and that which he sought for himself?

Only in the Rodin Museum at Meudon and in these old photographs can we realize that throughout his life Rodin worked daily in a sculptural environment that was mostly white. The moment a work was finished in clay, it went into plaster, and even if cast in bronze, it was the plasters that remained in the studio. (Bronzes were invariably cast on demand and not stored in the studio on speculation.) We tend to look upon plaster as a second-class artistic medium, a half-way house *en route* to bronze or stone. Rodin once referred to clay as representing life; plaster he equated with death and marble with resurrection. Yet he exhibited, sold and gave away plasters, urging their purchase upon discriminating collectors and those who, like Mrs Adolph Spreckels of San Francisco, would build public collections of his art. Plasters helped Rodin keep his options open while giving him permanence. The matt rather than glossy finish of the old photographs equates with that of the plasters and permitted Rodin and his photographers close study of detail and nuance without distractions from reflecting surfaces. Shadows on plasters could be as luminous as those on marbles.

The old prints also capture the abundant life Rodin created in his studios, into which he could immerse himself and from which he drew fresh inspiration, much as Henry Moore does to this day. By seeing sculptures juxtaposed in the studio, we are reminded of how Rodin's art helped to breed itself. He may have spent as much if not more time manipulating his plasters, seeking their fruitful friction or effecting new grafts of limbs and bodies, as he did in working directly from the model. He did this with drawings, sometimes cutting out figures, putting them in frieze-like compositions, or just having piles of them available for auditions when the spirit moved him. This adamant apostle of working directly from nature not only relied upon memory of things observed, but by means of the plasters allowed his imagination full play to create what had never been seen. His creativity thus did not rest on modelling alone, but also on manipulation of his 'readymades'. As did Picasso later, Rodin believed in economy of effort to relieve creativity of certain burdensome acts, especially as he grew older. From the beginning, however, when in full possession of his considerable energy, he determined never to let a good piece of modelling, such as the *Man with the Broken Nose*, be limited to one existence. A sculpture's renewability was limited only by Rodin's lifespan.

The *éminence blanche* in Rodin's studios and life was *The Gates of Hell* (Plate 18). Repeatedly, Rodin had his photographers pose sculptures before it, as if the great denuded portal were a light reflector. Behind these sculptures appear tantalizing glimpses of sections of the door (Plates 13, 95), usually, but not always, stripped of figures in high relief. For reasons of his own and with only two known exceptions, Rodin seems not to have encouraged photographs of his plaster 'Noah's Ark' with all its figures in place. The first photographs we have of this epic project intact were taken in the year after his death when *The Gates* were reassembled.

Even before the portal had begun to take on its inhabitants, Rodin's practice of using just its bare wooden armature as a backdrop for photographs of *The Thinker* and *Ugolino* in clay give us an idea of how it was made (Plates 19, 21, 22, 27). He erected in the government-supplied studio at the Dépôt des Marbres a simple armature of plain boards, nailed horizontally to a vertical framework that divided the central panels from the side reliefs. The lintel area was at first shallow and seems to have curved upward at one time. In the background of a photograph of *Eternal Spring* (Plate 48) can be made out the lower mouldings of the door modelled in clay applied directly to the wood. It seems likely that Rodin roughed out the overall vertical surface of the doors in clay and then made plaster casts of the sections. These casts, which were in turn mounted on a new armature, can today be seen at Meudon. Thus, these old photographs are of incomparable archaeological value.

It was customary for an artist to exhibit publicly a plaster with a 'Salon finish', realized in every detail, but awaiting a future patron's decision on the final medium. Rodin had successfully observed this practice and won government commissions to cast his *Age of*

Bronze and *Saint John the Baptist*, among others. The Rodin we never saw was the artist who boldly used the Salon as an extension of his atelier, doing in public what artists were enjoined to restrict to the privacy of the studio. A photograph taken in the Salon of 1897 in the gallery of the Palais de l'Industrie, hung with cotton tenting, shows the rudely mounted enlargement of *Victor Hugo and the Muses* (Plate 89). The parts of the author's figure were fresh from Lebossé's enlarging machines and their plaster casting. The straps used by Rodin's assistants to hold the extended left arm to the shoulder are undisguised, and there is an unclosed gap between them. The iron armature and upright bar that supports the hand might have been excused by those who knew the composition was intended for carving in stone. Rodin's refusal to be inhibited by conventions of perfection and finish are as dramatically seen in contemporary photographs taken by Druet and Bulloz of the major figural pieces exhibited in the salons after 1905: the *Seated Woman* (or *Cybele*), shown in 1905 and 1914 (Plate 128), *Reclining Woman* (or *Ariadne*), 1905 Plate 127), *The Walking Man*, 1907 (Plates 132–4), *Prayer* (Plate 130) and *Torso of a Young Woman* in 1910 (Plate 129), and *Châtiment* (or *Punishment*) of 1913 (Plate 131), all of which are partial figures and enlargements of work done before 1900. As early as 1886 in the Exposition Internationale and at the Georges Petit Gallery, he had shown a number of partial figures, listed as '*études*' or '*torses*'. The sculpture that served as the frontispiece of his 1900 exhibition, as shown in old photographs, was a partial figure of one of *The Burghers of Calais*. Of all Rodin's audacities, it was the partial figure, made famous partly through photography, that had the most immediate and tangible influence on the young revolutionaries of modern sculpture at the beginning of this century.

Photography and Rodin's Pygmalion dream

Rodin may have never tripped a shutter, but these old photographs give us an unprecedented intimacy with the artist and his work. How many sculptors before or since have used the camera as extensively and imaginatively? Photography helped him educate the public into art's work, while taking the mystery out of the studio and documenting artistic daring that transcended manual skill. Rodin used this relatively new medium not just as a record of things done, but as part of creation. Photographers became extensions of his eyes just as *practiciens* were surrogates for his hands; and prints, like plasters, could fix states in a sculpture's evolution and allow a return for a new departure. Actual drawing on prints tied photography to his mobility of thought and fed his editorial compulsions. Nothing, including photography, was unalterable. Art, like nature, meant perpetual self-renewal and self-surpassing effort.

Whatever photographers may have taught Rodin, they themselves learned even more from this 'demon of the best'. 'Mere exactitude' was not enough. Under his critical scrutiny photographers kept their individuality but learned to see his sculptures as living beings – in the round and dependent upon light and air. Interpretative photography was thereby enhanced. Compare the photographs of Rodin's art, such as Haweis and Coles's *Kneeling Faun*, with a photograph made for the academic sculptor, Falguière (who based some of his art on photos), and posed for by an École des Beaux-Arts model. The sculpture

The Kneeling Faun. Plaster, before 1884. Photo Haweis and Coles, gelatin silver print, 22.5 × 16.5 cm (cat. no. 1377)

École des Beaux-Arts model in an 'académie' or beauty pose, possibly in Falguière's studio. Date unknown. Photo Falguière?, 22.5 × 15.3 cm (cat. no. 1362)

is more alive. By training, the models posed as statues, and photographers took them as reliefs. Rodin and his photographers strove for the natural. Why else did Rodin love looking at his work not just indoors by daylight, but photographed at twilight in his gardens or in a meadow by moonlight? Why at times did he exhibit sculptures without bases, show his *Balzac* looking out of the window or as if pacing in a meadow (Plate 114), and push his bronze *Eve* (Plate 26) into a shadowed corner? Why so many views of figures partially illuminated, silhouetted against the light, or in soft focus, which mutes their identity as sculptures? Why the gum prints that suppress evidence of touch and sculptural drawing? Was it purely accidental that photographers recorded *President Sarmiento* (Plate 76) standing in an alley as if rehearsing a speech he would give in a few moments or that a battered medieval burgher (Plate 72) is shown reflecting before a monument to a modern hero? Was it lost upon Rodin that the courtyard of the Dépôt des Marbres served as a backdrop for love among the ruins in the form of an old crone's embrace by a naked adolescent (Plate 49)? Why all of this if not to make his art seem more real? Rodin once praised Steichen's work by saying that he 'would make the world understand my *Balzac* through his pictures. They are like Christ walking through the desert.' In the years when many photographers were interested in making photography look more like art, Rodin at times wanted the camera to project his vision of sculpture as one with life. Photography was yet another means by which this dramatist could stage his art and this self-styled 'worker' could be an artist.

Rodin seated in his dining room at Meudon. 1912? Photographer unknown, gelatin silver print, 15.6 × 20.6 cm (cat. no. 1346)

The Plates

NOTE ON THE PHOTOGRAPHIC PRINTS

One of the best sources on the technical nature and history of photographic prints is the book by Helmut and Alison Gernsheim, *The History of Photography, 1685–1914*, published by McGraw-Hill. The following information is drawn from the Gernsheims' book.

Albumen prints. Albumen prints developed from the process of making glass negatives in which the glass plate was coated with a thin layer of egg white containing a few drops of solution of iodide of potassium. After drying, the plate was washed with an acid solution of nitrate of silver. When the plate had been exposed, the latent image was developed with gallic acid. Recipes were like those in cookbooks, and it was a tedious process for the photographer. The process was invented by Abel Niepce de Saint-Victor in 1847. 'Albumen was found not only a convenient medium for the coating of glass negatives, but was also employed for coating positive paper. The originator of albumen paper was Blanquart-Evrard, 1850.' Albumen paper replaced silver chloride paper and gave a greater sharpness of image. It was often toned with chloride of gold to give various shades of brown. The drawback of this paper, as can be seen in some of Bodmer's prints, is its susceptibility to fading.

Gum-bichromate printing. The following is from an article in *The Photo-Miniature, A Magazine of Photographic Information*, Vol. 11, No. 22, January 1901:

What is a gum print? . . . it is a print made in gum and pigment by the help of potassium (or ammonium) bichromate. The gum may be almost any colloid substance, as white of egg, glue, gelatine, mucilage, gum arabic, etc. The pigment may be any insoluble water color, such as lamp black, umber, ochre, or the colors in pans or tubes used by water colorists. The potassium (or ammonium) bichromate is used in a 20 per cent solution. These three ingredients are properly combined and spread on a suitable paper. When the coating is dry the paper is exposed in a printing frame through a negative, just as any other photographic paper is exposed. Now the sunlight acts on the gum in the presence of the bichromate, rendering the former insoluble in proportion to the amount of light action. Thus, under the thinnest or least opaque parts of the negative nearly all the gum is

made insoluble, while under the thick or dense portions, in the high lights, the gum remains more or less soluble. The paper is now removed from the printing frame and washed in water with proper precautions, and with certain necessary but simple manipulations. The soluble gum softens and is washed away, taking the pigment with it and leaving the paper clear in the high lights. The gum, which has been rendered insoluble, holds to the paper, retaining the pigment, and giving the darker parts of the picture.

Gelatin silver bromide paper. This type of paper, the most frequently encountered among the photographic prints in this book, was invented and first produced in 1873 by Peter Mawdsley, and the solution was used for both negatives and positive copies. 'An exposure to a few seconds of gas or other artificial light was sufficient – it had advantage for direct enlargement. . . . The essential qualities of bromide papers were, and remain, their speed and the ease with which either contact prints or direct enlargement can be obtained by artificial light in a few seconds, and the absolute uniformity of the results.' Papers coated with gelatine chloride could also be given a burnt sienna tint and were superior in permanence to albumen paper.

Salt prints. Sodium chloride or salt prints were invented by Fox Talbot in 1834. Salt was added to silver chloride, and there followed a succession of salt and silver washes to fix the image.

The Gernsheims record that the process was invented by Poitevin in the 1850s, and in 1894 it was introduced by A. Rouille-Ladêvese and popularized a year later by Robert Demachy. 'It enabled the photographer to control the printing, omit details, change tone and values, and by a great variety of manipulations to modify the photograph to such an extent that it became the result of hand work far removed from the original camera image . . . the picture could be given the appearance of a red chalk or charcoal drawing.'

1. *Mask of the Man with the Broken Nose*. Bronze, 1863–4. Photo Druet, gelatin silver print, 39.8 × 29.8 cm (cat. no. 1439)

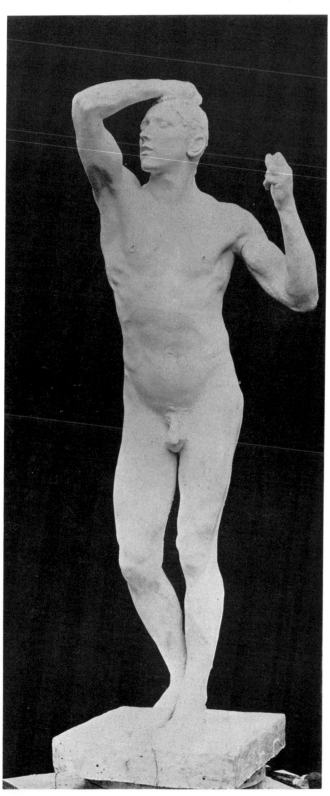

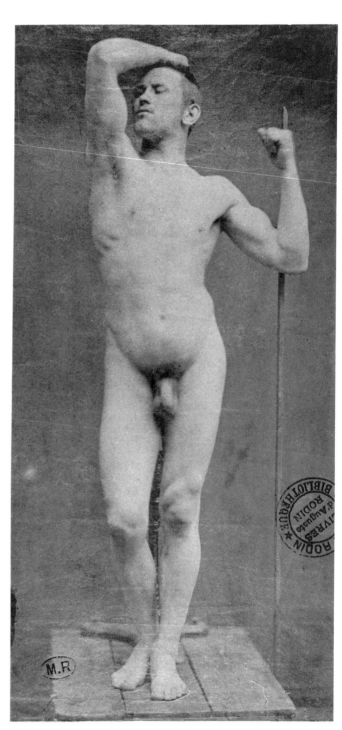

2. *The Age of Bronze* (front view). Plaster, 1875–6.
Photo Marconi, albumen print, 26.3 × 16 cm (cat. no. 1424)

3. Auguste Neyt (front view). 1877.
Photo Marconi?, albumen print, 24 × 14.8 cm (cat. no. 1359)

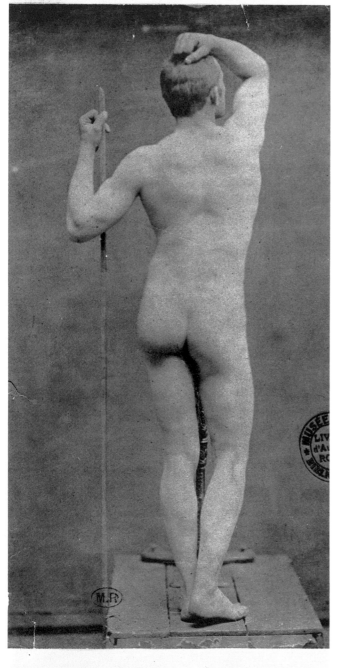

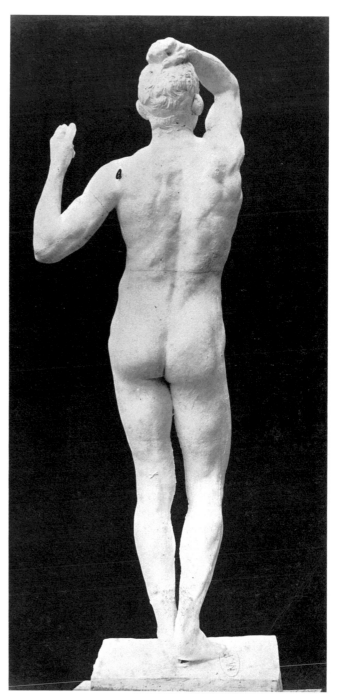

4. Auguste Neyt (back view). 1877.
Photo Marconi?, albumen print, 25.3 × 15 cm (cat. no. 1358)

5. *The Age of Bronze* (back view). Plaster, 1875–6.
Photo Marconi, albumen print, 26.2 × 13.7 cm (cat. no. 1445)

7. *Seated Ugolino* (side view). Plaster, 1877.
Photo (taken in 1900) Bodmer or Pannelier?, gelatin silver print with
ink notations, 26 × 20.4 cm (cat. no. 1425)

8 (below). *Seated Ugolino* (side view). Plaster, 1877.
Photo Bodmer or Pannelier?, gelatin silver print, 14.5 × 10 cm (cat.
no. 1371)

6 (opposite). *Seated Ugolino* (back view). Plaster, 1877.
Photo Bodmer or Pannelier?, albumen print with ink notations,
17 × 12.9 cm (cat. no. 1343)

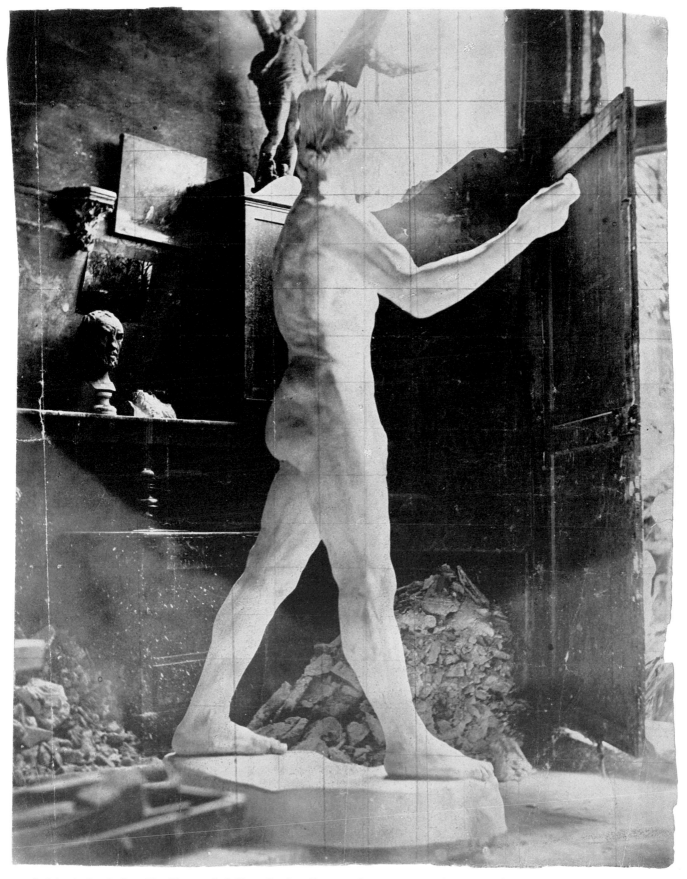

10. *St John the Baptist Preaching*. Plaster, 1878. Photo Freuler, albumen print, 14.2 × 11 cm (cat. no. 1335)

9 (opposite). *St John the Baptist Preaching* (without hand). Plaster, 1878.
Photo Freuler, albumen print, 17.4 × 12.4 cm (cat. no. 1352)

11. *St John the Baptist Preaching* (front view). Plaster, 1878. Photo Braun?, albumen print, 30 × 24 cm (cat. no. 1417)

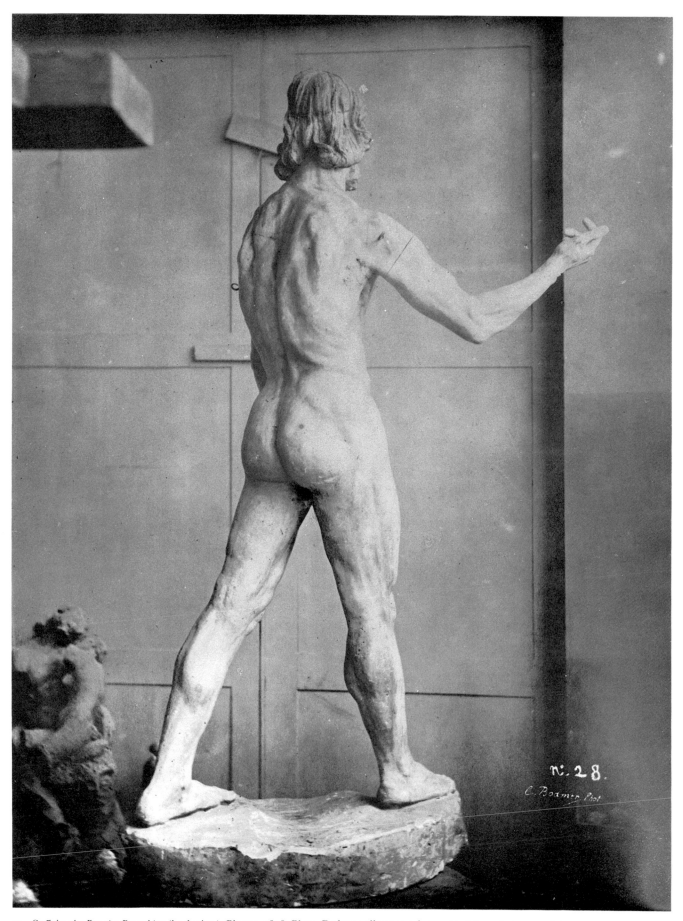

12. *St John the Baptist Preaching* (back view). Plaster, 1878. Photo Bodmer, albumen print, 25 × 18.6 cm (cat. no. 1380)

13. *La Défense*. Bronze, 1879; enlarged version seen here, *c.* 1899. Photo Druet, gelatin silver print, 38.4 × 28.4 cm (cat. no. 1467)

14. The Trocadéro Fountain. *c.* 1878. Photographer unknown, albumen print, 27.4 × 39 cm (cat. no. 1487)

15. *Bellona*. Bronze, 1878. Photo (taken in 1900) Druet, gelatin silver print, 39.6 × 30 cm (cat. no. 1398)

16. *Head of Rose*. Plaster, 1880–2. Photographer unknown, albumen print, 25.8 × 19.9 cm (cat. no. 1444)

17. The third architectural model for *The Gates of Hell*. Plaster, 1880. Photo Bodmer?, albumen print with pencil additions, 20 × 10.7 cm (cat. no. 1361)

18. *The Gates of Hell.* Plaster, 1880–1917. Photo (taken in 1900) Druet?, gelatin silver print, 26.7 × 20.2 cm (cat. no. 1383).
Inscribed on the photograph by Rodin in ink: 'Moins grosses de dimensions/les moulures/plus incolores/plus fines'

19. *The Thinker*. Clay, 1880–1. Photo Pannelier or Bodmer?, albumen print with pencil notations, 24 × 11.5 cm (cat. no. 1345)

20. *The Thinker*. Clay, 1880–1. Photo Pannelier or Bodmer?, albumen print, 14.5 × 10.1 cm (cat. no. 1355)

22. *The Thinker* (on a scaffolding). Clay, 1880–1. Photo Pannelier or Bodmer?, gelatin silver print, 14.5 × 10.2 cm (cat. no. 1369)

21. *The Thinker* (on a scaffolding). Clay, 1880–1. Photo Pannelier or Bodmer?, gelatin silver print, 14.5 × 10 cm (cat. no. 1370)

23. *The Thinker*. Bronze, enlargement of 1904? Photographer unknown, gelatin silver print, 35 × 25 cm (cat. no. 1428)

24. *The Thinker*. Bronze, 1904? Photographer unknown, gum print, 40.7 × 25.3 cm (cat. no. 1493)

25. *Eve* (side view). Bronze, 1881. Photo Druet, gelatin silver print, 40 × 29.8 cm (cat. no. 1483)

26. *Eve* (back view). Bronze, 1881. Photo Druet, gelatin silver print, 38.6 × 28.5 cm (cat. no. 1494)

27 (left). *Ugolino and his Sons* (second version, penultimate stage). Clay, 1880–1? Photographer unknown, albumen print with pencil notations, 20 × 16.8 cm (cat. no. 1470)

29 (opposite). *Ugolino and his Sons* (third version). Plaster, after 1889. Photographer unknown, gelatin silver print, 18 × 13 cm (cat. no. 1478)

28 (below). *Ugolino and his Sons* (second version, final stage). Clay, 1880–1? Photographer unknown, albumen print, 11 × 15.5 cm (cat. no. 1347)

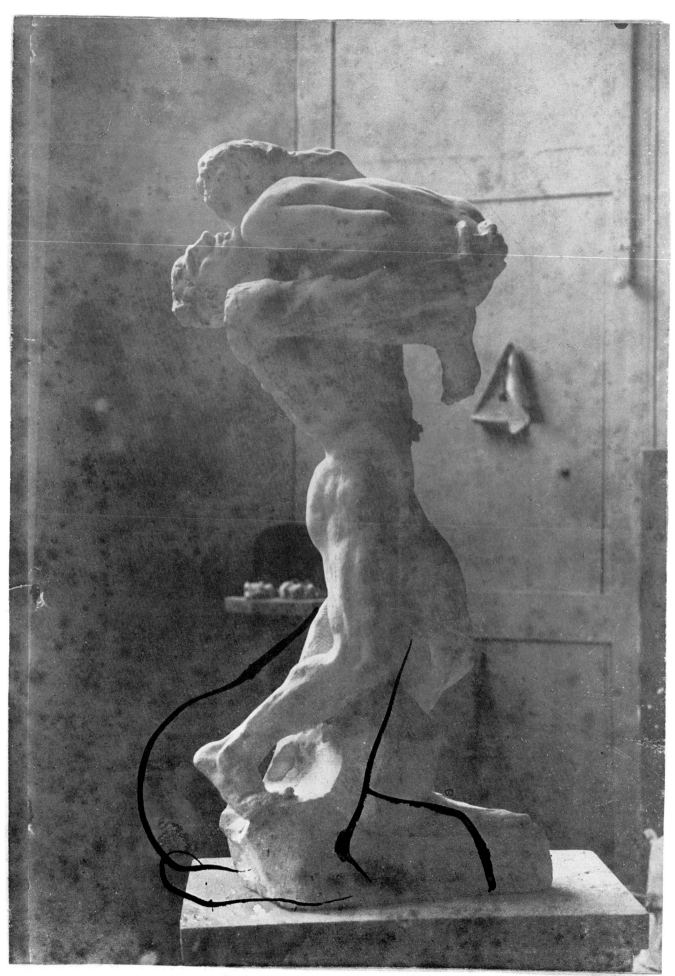

30. *'I Am Beautiful'* (*'Je Suis Belle'*). Plaster, 1882. Photo Bodmer, albumen print with ink additions, 16.6 × 11.9 cm (cat. no. 1363)

31. *The Crouching Woman*. Clay, 1880–1. Photo Bodmer, albumen print, 16.6 × 11.7 cm (cat. no. 1357)

33. *Fugitive Love*. Plaster?, before 1887. Photo Bodmer?, albumen print, 12.7 × 16.9 cm (cat. no. 1342)

32 (opposite). *Fugitive Love*. Plaster?, 1881? Photo Bodmer?, albumen print, 17 × 12.2 cm (cat. no. 1372)

34. *Fallen Caryatid Carrying her Stone*. Bronze, 1881. Photographer unknown, double-coated print with pencil hatchings, 29.5 × 24 cm (cat. no. 1420)

35. *Fallen Caryatid Carrying her Stone*. Bronze, 1881. Photographer unknown, gum print, 29.5 × 23.3 cm (cat. no. 1421)

36. *The Shade*. Plaster, enlarged version 1898? Photo Bulloz, gelatin silver print, 35.6 × 25.3 cm (cat. no. 1431)

37. *The Shade with the Fallen Caryatid*. Plaster, after 1898. Photo Bodmer, gelatin silver print, 17 × 12 cm (cat. no. 1354)

38. *Meditation* or *The Inner Voice*. Plaster, 1885 or 1896–7. Photo Freuler, salt print, 24.1 × 18 cm (cat. no. 1394)

39. *The Shade with Meditation*. Plaster, after 1898. Photo Bodmer, gelatin silver print, 38.3 × 27.2 cm (cat. no. 1397)

40. *The Martyr* (mounted on an armature). Plaster, 1885.
Photographer unknown, gelatin silver print, 23.6 × 17.7 cm
(cat. no. 1385)

41. *The Martyr* or *The Broken Lily*. Rough cut in stone, 1910?
Photographer unknown, gelatin silver print, 24 × 18 cm (cat.
no. 1393)

42. *The Martyr* or *The Broken Lily*. Fine cut in stone, 1911. Photo Druet, gelatin silver print, 38.5 × 28.5 cm (cat. no. 1480)

43. *Icarus*. Marble, 1895? Photo Druet, gelatin silver print, 21.1 × 31 cm (cat. no. 1403)

44. Enlarged torso of *The Martyr*. Plaster, 1898? Photo Druet?, gelatin silver print, 38.3 × 28 cm (cat. no. 1396)

45. *Madame Alfred Roll*. Plaster and clay, 1882 or 1883. Photographer unknown, albumen print, 23 × 17.2 cm (cat. no. 1376)

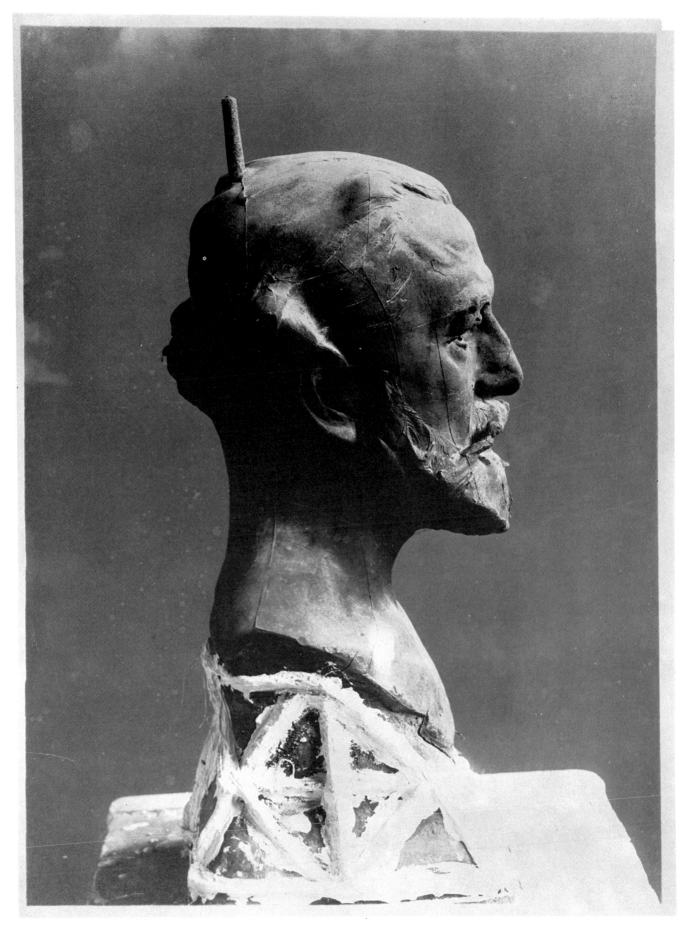

46. *Antonin Proust*. Clay or bronze?, 1884. Photo Bulloz, gelatin silver print, 34.6 × 25.4 cm (cat. no. 1438)

47. Auguste Rodin, photograph taken in 1880. Photographer unknown, albumen print, 21.8 × 16.8 cm (cat. no. 1375)

48. *Eternal Spring* (*The Gates of Hell* in clay in the background). Clay, 1881? Photo Bodmer, albumen print, 19 × 24.3 cm (cat. no. 1389)

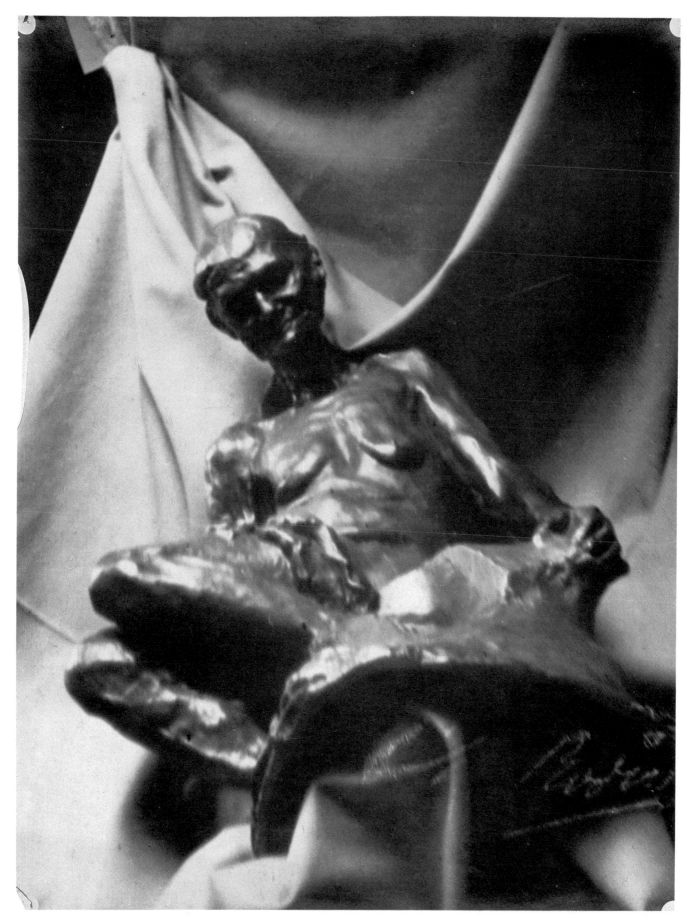

49. *The Helmet-Maker's Wife* or *The Old Courtesan*. Bronze, 1880–3. Photo Druet, gelatin silver print, 39.7 × 30 cm (cat. no. 1400)

50. *Triumphant Youth*. Plaster, 1894. Photo Druet, gelatin silver print, 25 × 18.8 cm (cat. no. 1491)

51. *Eustache de St Pierre*. Clay, 1886. Photo
Pannelier, albumen print with ink drawing,
37.7 × 16.7 cm (cat. no. 1447)

52. *Eustache de St Pierre*.
Clay, 1886. Photo Pannelier,
albumen print?, 35 × 20.2 cm
(cat. no. 1450)

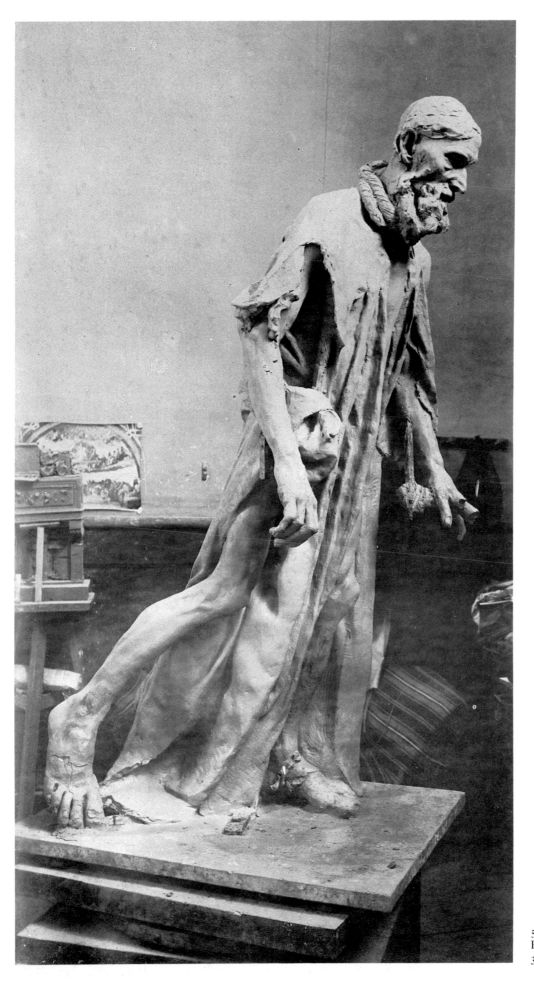

53. *Eustache de St Pierre.* Clay, 1886
Photo Pannelier, albumen print?,
37.7 × 19.4 cm (cat. no. 1455)

54. *Eustache de St Pierre*. Clay, 1886. Photo Pannelier, albumen print?, 39.2 × 18 cm (cat. no. 1452)

55. *Pierre de Wiessant* (so-called). Clay, 1886. Photo Bodmer, albumen print?, 25.3 × 21.5 cm (cat. no. 1401)

56. *Pierre de Wiessant* (so-called). Clay, 1886. Photo Bodmer, albumen print?, 24 × 21.5 cm (cat. no. 1402)

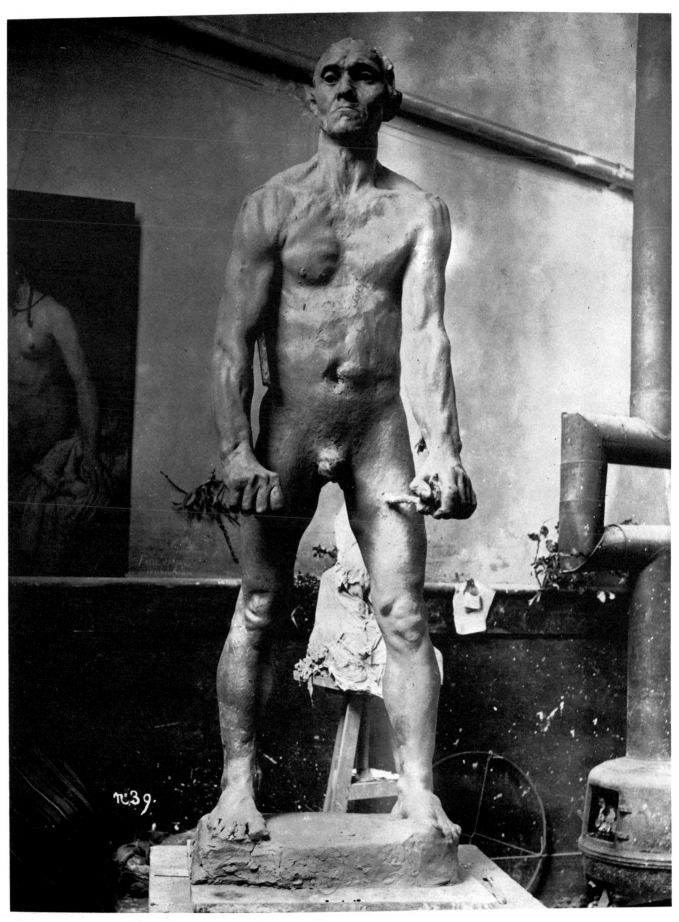

57. *Jean d'Aire* (naked). Clay, 1886. Photo Bodmer, albumen print, 25 × 19 cm (cat. no. 1390)

58. *Jean d'Aire* (robed). Clay, 1886. Photo Pannelier, albumen print, 41 × 18 cm (cat. no. 1457)

60. *The Burghers of Calais.* Final arrangement, 1889? Photographer unknown, gum print, 29.4 × 39 cm (cat. no. 1489)

59 (opposite). *Burgher of Calais, with his Head in his Hands.* Clay, 1886. Photo Pannelier, albumen print, 34.5 × 20 cm (cat. no. 1453)

61. *The Burghers of Calais.* Final arrangement, 1889? Photographer unknown, gum print, 38.8 × 28.5 cm (cat. no. 1476)

62. *The Burghers of Calais.* Final arrangement, 1889? Photographer unknown, gum print, 40 × 28.8 cm (cat. no. 1469)

63. *The Burghers of Calais.* Final arrangement, 1889? Photographer unknown, gum print, 30 × 39.5 cm (cat. no. 1475)

64 (opposite). *The Burghers of Calais.* Final arrangement, 1889? Photographer unknown, gum print, 38 × 26.8 cm (cat. no. 1405)

65. *The Clenched Hand* or *The Expressive Hand* (masked with a blanket). Bronze, 1885? Photo Druet, gelatin silver print, 29.9 × 39.7 cm (cat. no. 1407)

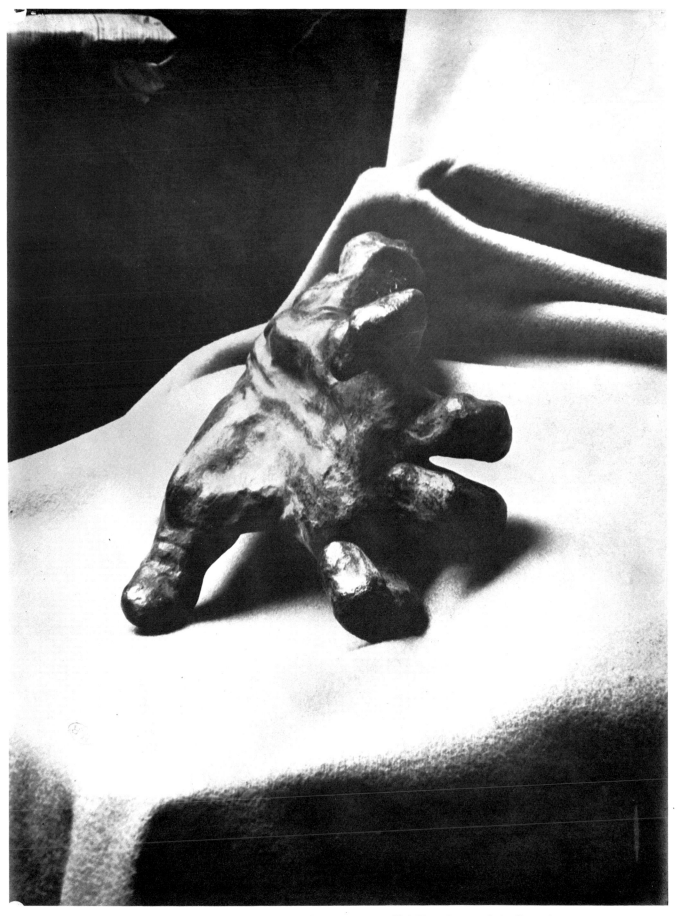

66. *The Clenched Hand* or *The Expressive Hand* (masked with a blanket). Bronze, 1885? Photo Druet, gelatin silver print, 39.8 × 30 cm (cat. no. 1482)

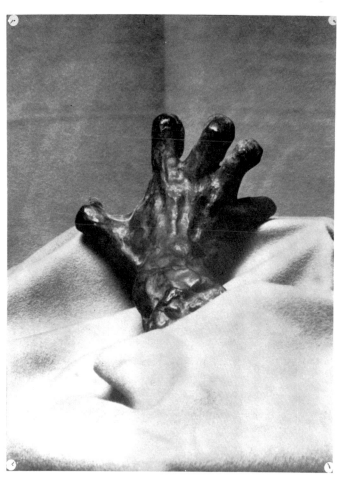

67 (left). *The Clenched Hand* or *The Expressive Hand* (masked with a blanket). Bronze, 1885? Photo Druet, gelatin silver print, 40 × 30 cm (cat. no. 1408)

68 (below). *The Clenched Hand* or *The Expressive Hand* (masked with a blanket). Bronze, 1885? Photo Druet, gelatin silver print, 30 × 40 cm (cat. no. 1406)

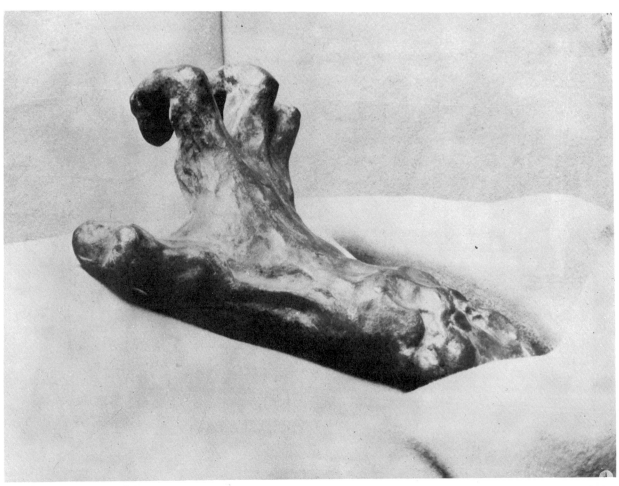

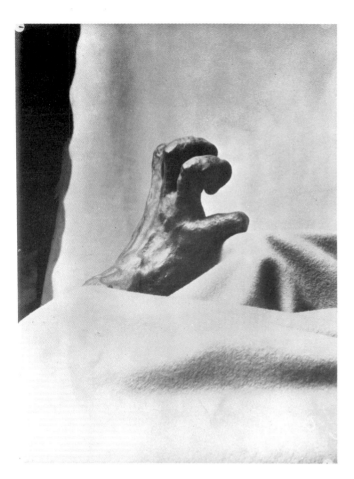

69 (left). *The Clenched Hand* or *The Expressive Hand* (masked with a blanket). Bronze, 1885? Photo Druet, gelatin silver print , 40 × 30 cm (cat. no. 1409)

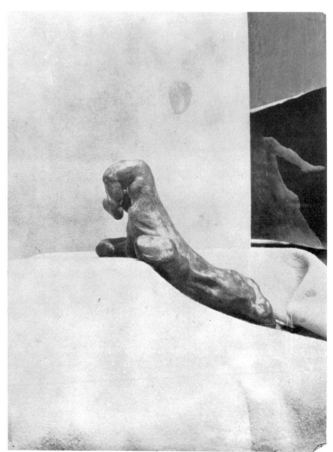

70 (right). *The Clenched Hand* or *The Expressive Hand* (masked with a blanket). Bronze, 1885? Photo Druet, gelatin silver print, 40 × 30 cm (cat. no. 1411)

71. *Faun and Satyr*. Clay, 1886. Photo Bodmer, albumen print, 16.8 × 20 cm (cat. no. 1374)

72. Model for a *Monument to Benjamin Vicuña-McKenna* (Eustache de St Pierre in the background). Clay, 1886. Photo Bodmer, albumen print with ink drawing, 25 × 18.8 cm (cat. no. 1391)

73. The *Monument to Claude Lorrain*. Plaster, 1889? Photo Freuler, salt print with ink corrections, 26.7 × 18 cm (cat. no. 1387)

74. Base of the *Monument to Claude Lorrain*. Marble, 1889? Photo Freuler, albumen print, 25.7 × 18.4 cm (cat. no. 1488)

75. *Claude Lorrain*. Bronze, 1889? Photo Michelez, albumen print with ink drawing, 33.5 × 22.3 cm (cat. no. 1451)

76. *President Sarmiento*. Bronze, 1896. Photo Druet, gelatin silver print, 39.8 × 29.7 cm (cat. no. 1412)

77. *The Metamorphoses of Ovid*. Plaster, before 1886. Photographer unknown, albumen print with pencil drawing, 15 × 10.8 cm (cat. no. 1353)

78. *The Juggler* or *The Acrobat*. Bronze, 1892–5. Photo Druet, gelatin silver print, 39.8 × 29.8 cm (cat. no. 1410)

79. *Couple Seen from the Back*. Plaster, date unknown, possibly 1890s. Photo H. C. Ellis, gelatin silver print, 17 × 11.6 cm (cat. no. 1348)

80 (right). *A Night in May*. Plaster?, date unknown. Photographer unknown, gelatin silver print, 23 × 16.8 cm (cat. no. 1443)

82 (right). *Young Girl Kissed by a Phantom*. Plaster?, 1880s?
Photographer unknown, salt print with pencil drawing,
26 × 20 cm (cat. no. 1381)

81 (below). *Young Girl Kissed by a Phantom*. Plaster?, 1880s?
Photographer unknown, salt print with ink drawing,
20 × 26 cm (cat. no. 1382)

83. *Twilight and Dawn*. Plaster, date unknown, male figure 1882. Photo Bodmer?, albumen print with gouache,
10 × 14.4 cm (cat. no. 1350)

l'aurore Contrepartie du Crepuscu...

84. *Twilight and Dawn*. Plaster, date unknown, male figure 1882. Photo Bodmer?, albumen print with gouache, 12.2 × 17 cm (cat. no. 1373)

86. *Victor Hugo*. Clay, 1883. Photo Bodmer, albumen print with
pencil drawing, 14 × 10.2 cm (cat. no. 1368)

85. *Victor Hugo*. Clay, 1883. Photo Bodmer, albumen print,
14.5 × 10 cm (cat. no. 1367)

87. *Victor Hugo*. Clay, 1883. Photo Bodmer, gelatin print with pencil drawing, 13.8 × 10.5 cm (cat. no. 1366)

88. *Victor Hugo* (Rodin in the background). Clay, 1883. Photo Bodmer, gelatin print, 13.5 × 10.5 cm (cat. no. 1365)

89. The *Monument to Victor Hugo: Victor Hugo and the Muses.* Plaster, 1897. Photographer unknown, gelatin silver print, 23.2 × 29.8 cm (cat. no. 1426)

90 (opposite). Study for the *Monument to Victor Hugo.* Plaster, 1897? Photo Bulloz, gelatin silver print, 35.6 × 25.4 cm (cat. no. 1441)

91. *The Tragic Muse*. Plaster, before 1885. Photo Bulloz, gelatin silver print, 38.8 × 28.8 cm (cat. no. 1436)

92. *The Tragic Muse and a Son of Ugolino*. Plaster, after 1906. Photo Bulloz, gelatin silver print, 27.8 × 37.3 cm (cat. no. 1435)

93. *Despair* (foreshortened view). Bronze, 1890. Photo Druet, gelatin silver print, 40 × 30 cm (cat. no. 1448)

94. *Despair* (masked by a blanket). Bronze, 1890. Photo Druet, gelatin silver print, 39.5 × 29 cm (cat. no. 1465)

95. *Iris, Messenger of the Gods,* with *The Gates of Hell* in the background. Bronze, 1891. Photo Druet, gelatin silver print, 39 × 29.6 cm (cat. no. 1386)

96. *The Crouching Woman* (with the head of *Iris*). Plaster, *c.* 1913? Photo Druet, gelatin silver print, 23.7 × 33.7 cm (cat. no. 1459)

97. *The Kneeling Faun* (side view). Plaster, before 1884. Photo Bodmer, albumen print, 15.2 × 10.2 cm (cat. no. 1349)

98 (below). *The Kneeling Faun* (back view). Plaster, before 1884. Photo Bodmer, albumen print, 16.8 × 12 cm (cat. no. 1351)

99. *Orpheus and the Furies*. Plaster, 1884? Photographer unknown, gelatin silver print, 23.5 × 17.5 cm (cat. no. 1472)

101. *Orpheus and Eurydice Leaving Hell.* Plaster, before 1889. Photographer unknown, albumen print, 14.8 × 10.8 cm (cat. no. 1344)

102. *Orpheus and Eurydice Leaving Hell.* Marble, 1893. Photo Freuler, salt print, 25.4 × 17 cm (cat. no. 1384)

100 (opposite). *Orpheus Imploring the Gods.* Plaster, 1892? Photo Druet?, gelatin silver print, 35.6 × 25.5 cm (cat. no. 1415)

103. *Christ and Mary Magdalene*. Marble, 1903. Photo Bulloz, gelatin silver print with pencil correction, 35.3 × 25.7 cm (cat. no. 1461)

104. *The Hand of God*. Bronze, 1898? Photo Choumoff, gelatin silver print, 22.2 × 16.7 cm (cat. no. 1471)

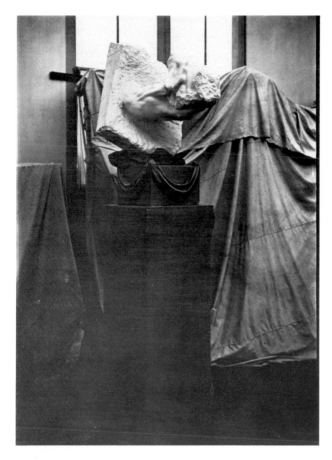

105. *The Hand of God* (shown as a relief). Stone, date unknown. Photographer unknown, gelatin silver print, 23.2 × 16.7 cm (cat. no. 1474)

106. *The Hand of God* (shown as a relief). Stone, date unknown. Photographer unknown, gelatin silver print, 23.5 × 19.5 cm (cat. no. 1392)

107. *Rodin with The Hand of God.* 1902? Photographer unknown, gelatin silver print, 11.9 × 16 cm (cat. no. 1326)

108. *The Kiss*. Marble, 1898. Photo Druet, gelatin silver print, 39.3 × 30 cm (cat. no. 1446)

109. *The Kiss*. Marble, 1898. Photo Druet, gelatin silver print, 39.8 × 29.7 cm (cat. no. 1477)

110. The *Monument to Balzac* in the Salon of 1898. Plaster. Photo Druet, gelatin silver print, 39.5 × 28.9 cm (cat. no. 1492)

112. Study of the robe for the *Monument to Balzac*. Plaster, 1897. Photo Freuler, salt print, 20.3 × 12 cm (cat. no. 1356)

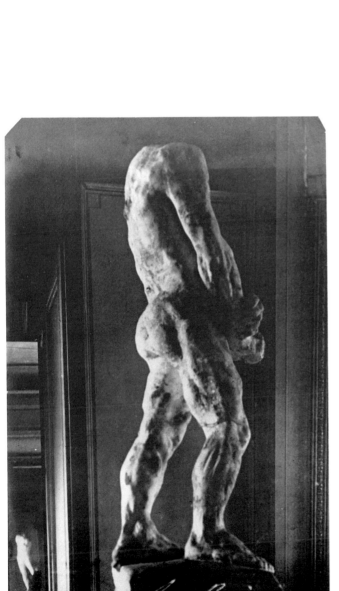

111. Figure study for the *Monument to Balzac*. Bronze, 1896–7. Photo Druet, gelatin silver print, 38.2 × 25.3 cm (cat. no. 1416)

113. *Balzac*, half-length version. Plaster, with pencil notations, 1897. Photo Druet, gelatin silver print, 39.5 × 29.8 cm (cat. no. 1399)

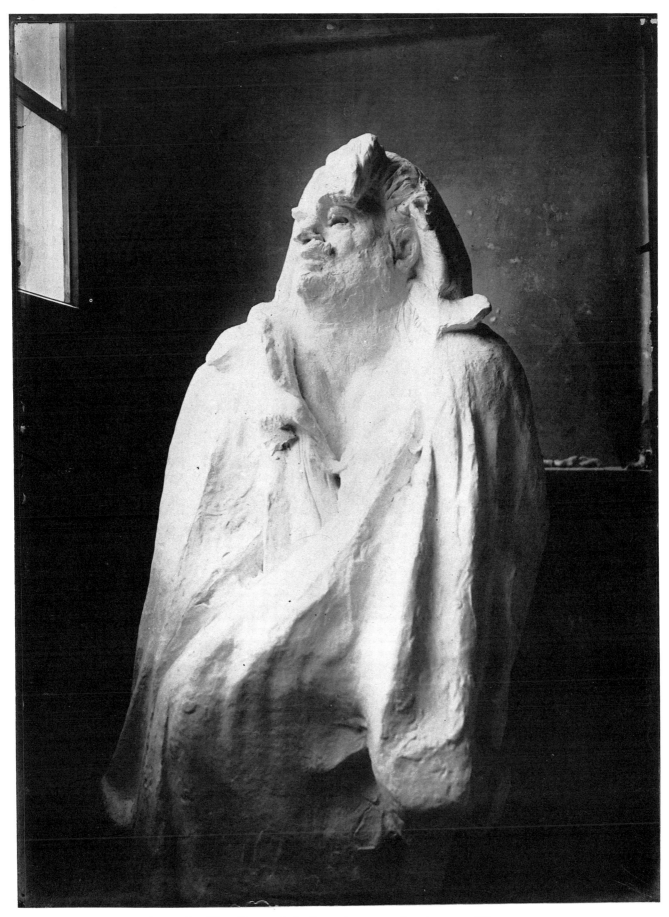

114. *Balzac*, by a window. Plaster, 1897. Photo Druet, gelatin silver print, 39 × 29.6 cm (cat. no. 1486)

115. The *Monument to Balzac* (seen at Meudon). Plaster, 1897. Photo Bulloz, gelatin silver print, 35.8 × 26.5 cm (cat. no. 1449)

116. The *Monument to Balzac* (seen at Meudon). Plaster, 1897. Photo Bulloz, gelatin silver print, 35.5 × 24.1 cm (cat. no. 1413)

117. The *Monument to Balzac* (seen at night at Meudon). Plaster, 1897. Photo (taken in 1908) Steichen, gelatin silver print,
23.1 × 18 cm (cat. no. 1419)

118. Rodin working at night. Date unknown. Photo Steichen, gelatin silver print, 28.4 × 22 cm (cat. no. 1418)

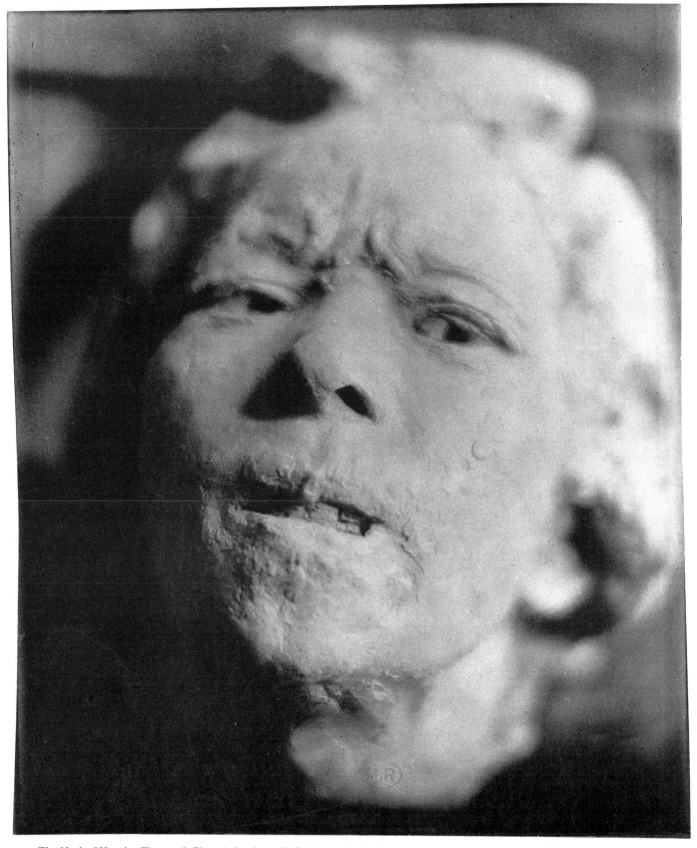

119. *The Mask of Hanako*. Clay, 1908. Photo (taken in 1908) Steichen, gelatin silver print, 24.5 × 20 cm (cat. no. 1388)

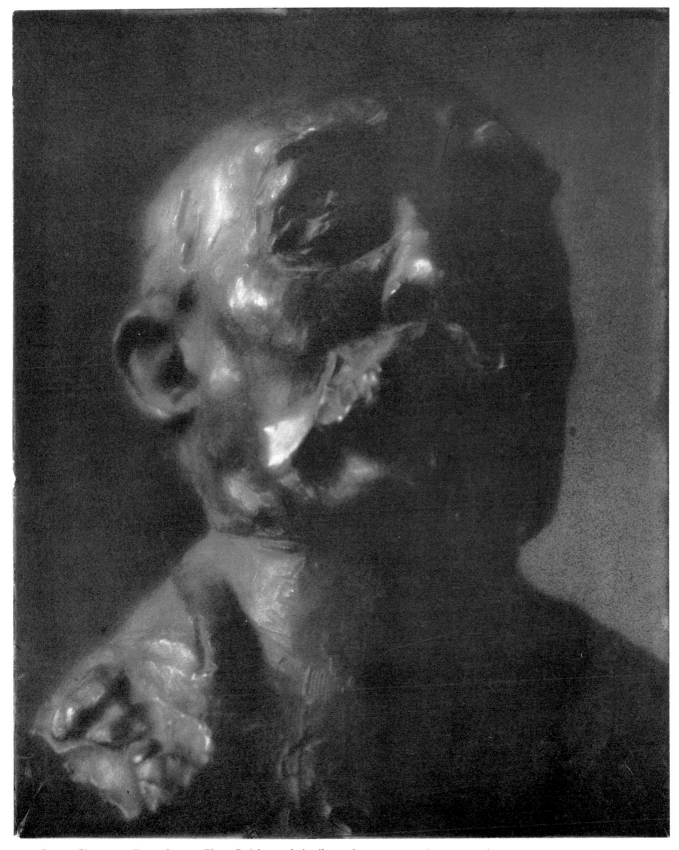

120. *Georges Clemenceau*. Bronze?, 1911. Photo Steichen, gelatin silver print, 25 × 20 cm (cat. no. 1404)

121. *The Head of Sorrow*, or *Joan of Arc*. Marble, 1907. Photo Bulloz, gelatin silver print, 35 × 27 cm (cat. no. 1432)

122. *Eve Fairfax*, or *The Amazon*. Marble, 1905? Photo Bulloz, gelatin silver print, 31.6 × 26.5 cm (cat. no. 1440)

123. *Barbey d'Aurevilly*. Plaster and clay, 1909. Photo World's Graphic Press, gelatin silver print, 35.6 × 25.3 cm (cat. no. 1341)

124. *Barbey d' Aurevilly*. Plaster and clay, 1909. Photo World's Graphic Press, gelatin silver print, 31.6 × 26.5 cm (cat. no. 1340)

125. The proposed *Monument to Puvis de Chavannes*. Plaster, 1899–*c*. 1907. Gelatin silver print, 23.7 × 17.5 cm (cat. no. 1473)

126. The Muse for the *Monument to Whistler*. Plaster, 1905–10. Photo Bulloz, gelatin silver print, 36.5 × 26.5 cm (cat. no. 1468)

127. *Ariadne*, or *Reclining Woman* (seen in foreshortening in the Salon of 1905?). Plaster, enlarged version. Photo Bulloz, gelatin silver print,
25 × 19.4 cm (cat. no. 1429)

128. *Cybele*, or *Seated Woman* (enlarged version seen in the Salon of 1905). Plaster. Photo Bulloz, gelatin silver print, 35.5 × 25.5 cm (cat. no. 1463)

129. *Torso of a Young
Woman* (enlarged version
seen in the Salon of 1910).
Plaster. Photo Druet,
gelatin silver print,
35.4 × 20.7 cm (cat.
no. 1456)

130. *Prayer* (enlarged version seen
in the Salon of 1910). Plaster. Photo
Druet, gelatin silver print,
30 × 19 cm (cat. no. 1460)

131. *Punishment*, or *Châtiment* (back view, enlarged version seen in the Salon of 1912). Plaster. Photo Druet, gelatin silver print, 37 × 27.6 cm (cat. no. 1454)

132. *The Walking Man* (enlarged version, seen in the courtyard of the Farnese Palace in Rome, 1912). Bronze.
Photo Cesare Feraglia, gelatin silver print with ink notations, 25.6 × 20 cm (cat. no. 1422)

133. *The Walking Man* (enlarged version, seen in the courtyard of the Hôtel Biron in Paris). Bronze, 1907.
Photo Druet, gelatin silver print, 36 × 21.7 cm (cat. no. 1458)

134. *The Walking Man*. Bronze, 1912? Photo Haweis and Coles, gum print, 23.5 × 17 cm (cat. no. 1423)

135. *A couple.* Plaster, date unknown. Photographer unknown, gelatin silver print, 18.3 × 12.8 cm (Stanford University Art Museum)

136. *A couple in a small urn*. Plaster, date unknown. Photographer unknown, gelatin silver print 18.2 × 12.7 cm
(Stanford University Art Museum)

137. Rodin in his studio,
conversing. 1912? Photo Druet?,
albumen print, 17 × 23.9 cm (cat.
no. 1337)

As much as possible I have tried to give the views of Rodin and his contemporaries on each work. The authors on whom I have drawn for information in the entries are as follows:

Georges Grappe, *Catalogue du Musée Rodin*, 1944

John Tancock, *The Sculptures of Auguste Rodin*, Philadelphia Museum of Art, 1976

Jacques de Caso and Patricia Sanders, *Rodin's Sculpture*, The Fine Arts Museums of San Francisco, 1978

Athena Spear, *Rodin Sculptures in the Cleveland Museum of Art*, 1967, 1974

Ruth Butler Mirolli, *The Early Work of Rodin and its Background*, University Microfilms, 1966

Judith Cladel, *Rodin, sa vie glorieuse, sa vie inconnue*, Édition Définitive, Grasset, 1950

Paul Gsell, *Rodin on Art*, Horizon Press, 1971

Frederick Lawton, *The Life and Work of Auguste Rodin*, Unwin, 1906

Robert Descharnes and J.-F. Chabrun, *Auguste Rodin*, Macmillan, 1967

Three important essays on Rodin are contained in my anthology, *Auguste Rodin: Readings on his Life and Work*, Prentice Hall, 1965. They are: Truman H. Bartlett, 'Auguste Rodin, Sculptor'; Rainer Maria Rilke, 'Auguste Rodin'; and H. C. E. Dujardin-Beaumetz, 'Rodin's Reflections on Art'.

Measurements have not been given because the plasters differ slightly from the bronzes and marbles made after them, and the exact dimensions are not yet available. The words 'Meudon Reserve' refer to the storage area of the Rodin Museum at Meudon, just outside Paris. The new Rodin Museum Administration has embarked upon a programme of giving greater visibility to the many sculptures stored there for years, and undoubtedly these works will be available to the public in the future.

1. *Mask of the Man with the Broken Nose.* 1863–4.

This sculpture was originally called *Mask of a Man* and *The Broken Nose*. Done when he was twenty-three and twenty-four, it became Rodin's talisman:

> The mask determined all my future work. It is the first good piece of modelling I ever did. From that time I sought to look all around my work, to draw it well in every respect. I have kept that mask before my mind in everything I have done. I tried it on my first figure, *The Bacchante*, but did not succeed. I again tried it on *The Age of Brass* [*The Age of Bronze*], also without success, though it is a good figure. In fact, I have never succeeded in making a figure as good as *The Broken Nose*.

This statement was made to the American sculptor, Truman H. Bartlett, probably in 1888. Some twenty years later Rodin told Dujardin-Beaumetz: 'For tenacity in study, for sincerity in execution of form, I have never done more or better. I worked as completely as I could, thought of nothing else.'

In talking to Bartlett about the stable he used as a studio at the time, Rodin remembered: 'The winter that year was especially rude, and I couldn't have a fire at night. *The Man with the Broken Nose* froze. The back of the head split off and fell. I was able to save only the face.'

The subject, according to Bartlett, 'was made from a poor old man who picked up a precarious living in the neighborhood by doing odd jobs for anyone who would employ him and who went by the name of "Bébé".' Rodin explained his choice of subjects and his intention: 'He had a fine head; belonged to a fine race – in form – no matter if he was brutalized. It was made as a piece of sculpture, solely and without reference to the character of the model, as such. I called it *The Broken Nose*, because the nose of the model was broken.'

2–5. *The Age of Bronze.* 1875–6.

Today when sculptors have retrospectives before the age of thirty-five, it is astounding to realize that Rodin did not make his public début as a statue-maker, the most important title to which a sculptor could aspire, until the age of thirty-seven. To earn his bread he had been forced to leave France in 1871 for Belgium, and he worked for years in the employ of other sculptors or in collaboration with them, not signing his own name to his work. His agreement with Antoine van Rasbourg, the Belgian sculptor, stipulated that Rodin's name would only go on work exhibited outside Belgium. During a period when there was a shortage of work in Belgium, Rodin used his modest savings from his commercial enterprises to support himself for the eighteen months necessary to complete *The Age of Bronze*. He took a trip to Italy in 1875, interrupting work on the figure, to study Michelangelo at first hand. One of Rodin's most important qualities was patience, fortified by the belief, as he told young artisans in Belgium, that 'it is only necessary to make a single statue to establish a reputation.'

Rodin's model, a young Belgian soldier named Auguste Neyt, recalled his experience after the sculptor had selected him from among 'the best built' men in the company: 'I was at once introduced to his studio in the rue Sans-Souci in Ixelles, where I had to go through all kinds of poses every day in order to get the muscles right. Rodin did not want any exaggerated muscle, he wanted *naturalness*. I worked two, three and even four hours a day and sometimes for an hour at a stretch.'

Neyt was submitted to what Rodin considered a rigorous and exact scrutiny as part of a method he later described thus:

> I strive to express what I see with as much deliberation as I can. I proceed methodically by the study of the contours of the model which I copy, for it is important to rediscover in the work of art the strength and firmness of nature; translation of the human body in terms of the exactness of its contours gives shapes which are nervous, solid, abundant, and by itself [this method] makes life arise out of truth. . . . When I begin a figure I first look at the front, the back, the two profiles of right and left, that is their contours from four angles; then, with clay, I arrange the large mass as I see it and as exactly as possible. Then I do the intermediate perspectives, giving the three-quarters profiles, then, successively turning my clay and my model, I compare and refine them. . . . In a human body, the contour is given by the place where the body ends; thus it is the body which makes the shape. I place the model so that light, outlining it against a background, illuminates the contour. I execute it, I change my position and that of my model, and thus I

Study for the head of *The Age of Bronze*. Terracotta, half-lifesize, 1876? Meudon Reserve. Photo Bruno Jarret, 1979

see another contour, and so on successively all round the body. . . . It is important to look at the shapes from beneath and above, . . . to look down on the contours from above and see those which overhang, that is, to become aware of the density of the human body. Looking at a skull from above, I see the contours of the temples, the hollows, the nose, the jaws – all the cranial construction which is ovoid when seen from above. Next I see and compare with my clay the plane of the pectorals, the scapulas, the buttocks. I look at the springing of the muscles of the thighs; below, the planting of the feet on the floor. When I was working on *The Age of Brass*, I procured one of those ladders painters use for their big canvases; I climbed up and did what I could to make my model and my clay agree in foreshortening, and I looked at the contours from above. What I do might be called 'drawing in depth', for . . . it isn't possible to make something that looks flat.

One would expect that with such a system Rodin could have achieved his figure without too much difficulty, but he told Bartlett, 'I was in the deepest despair with that figure, and I worked so intensely on it, trying to get what I wanted, that there are at least four figures in it.'

Unlike his later full figures, such as the *John the Baptist*, *The Age of Bronze* does not seem to have been preceded by a series of preliminary and smaller figure studies. There is, however, in the reserve of the Rodin Museum at Meudon, a smaller than life-size study of the head and right arm in terracotta, which may be explained by the fact that Rodin seems to have departed most from the model in the area of the face, a conjecture that is only now possible because of the scandal evoked by the statue when it was first exhibited in Paris during the spring of 1877, and because of Rodin's attempt to vindicate himself. The precious photographs by a Brussels photographer named Marconi show the plaster that was exhibited first in January, 1877, at the Cercle Artistique in Brussels and then in April at the Paris Salon. Rodin's sculpture encountered a mixed reception. It seems to have caused a sensation among many artists from its 'pure art point of view' and its surpassing of the work of contemporary 'realists' who made 'servile copies'. There were critics and artists, however, who were dismayed by Rodin's 'failure' to explain the subject and who suspected that his uncompromising rigour of modelling from nature had really been achieved by life-casting.

Rodin first offered the work as *The Vanquished*, but had reportedly removed a spear and a fillet from the figure before its first showing. He used Marconi's photographs as the basis for two drawings, one of which showed the weapon, which had been a baton the model used in the studio to support his left hand. Judith Cladel interpreted *Le Vaincu* to mean 'glorification of tragic heroism that had touched his French heart'. The sculpture thus originally reflected Rodin the patriot, celebrating France's heroism in the defeat of 1870, a theme he was to repeat in the late 1870s in *La Défense* and one adopted by other French sculptors. When shown in Paris, the work

was retitled: *The Age of Bronze* or *The Vanquished*. The former name Rodin was later to explain as man awakening to his humanity, 'that is to say, one who is passing from the unconsciousness of primitive man into the age of understanding and love'. The equivocal nature of the sculpture's meaning and its pathetic heroism give it a theme which, along with its form, reflects a modern consciousness.

The accusation of having cast from life was an insult to Rodin's integrity which he never forgot, even though he was able in subsequent work to exonerate himself. (The detailed account of the 1877 scandal and Rodin's response is given in both Cladel and Tancock.) According to Bartlett, it was at the suggestion of the jury that Rodin requested Neyt to have himself photographed. Rodin showed the photographs to at least one of the eighty-one jurors, Falguière, who was to become a strong friend, but the jury's verdict was not overturned. We can now study the photographs against those of the plaster sculpture, as Rodin intended. Neyt conscientiously posed in exactly the right stance, aided by a baton and a model's stand, whose vertical pipe rises between his legs. The photographer, probably Marconi, cooperated by setting the camera at the approximate distance and angle from the model as in the photographs of the plaster. The reader might imagine that he or she is a juror in 1877 studying this evidence. Do the photographs vindicate Rodin or confirm the accusation of life-casting? Could a case be made that Rodin's profile method produced discernible differences from a life cast? Would you agree with one of the original jurors that 'Even if it is cast from nature, it's very beautiful; it should be accepted anyway'?

6–8. *Seated Ugolino*. 1877. Plaster. Rodin Museum, Meudon.

After the artist's death, this work was known only in the literature until the spring of 1977, when Patricia Elsen discovered its photographs in the Paris Rodin Museum archives, and I was able to identify the actual plaster in the Meudon Reserve.

Truman H. Bartlett wrote in 1889:

Among the large studies made by the sculptor in Brussels, in the development of his principles of composition, was a group called 'Ugolin', but he was not satisfied with it, and destroyed all save the body of the principal figure. This is one of the best examples of his large style of modelling.

Studying the actual plaster invites the thought that the head and extremities may never have been made and that Rodin was interested only in certain parts of the body of the model, who was running to fat. Bartlett quotes the comments of a young sculptor, an admirer and possibly an assistant to Rodin later, who told of visiting the sculptor's studio shortly after the affair of *The Age of Bronze* in 1877: 'But when he showed us the body of the "Ugolin", we were still more surprised, and hardly knew what to say. It looked a bit like Michelangelo, it was so large, lifelike, and ample in the character of its planes and modelling.'

We do not know when Rodin commenced work on the figure. In a letter he sent to Rose, probably in the summer of 1877, he laments his financial plight and says that the '*moleur* demands that I pay 150 francs for having cast my Ugolin, and I will not pay it'. He had the partial figure shipped to Paris, and, as is confirmed by both Cladel and his correspondence, it was not finished and 'a leg had not been cast'. The fact that it was still in clay in 1877 makes it certain that this seated torso was begun after Rodin's trip in 1875 to Italy, where he was exposed directly and extensively to the works of Michelangelo. The torso also relates in pose to Carpeaux's *Ugolino* and to his own drawings of the theme. In 1874, for the Palais des Académies in Brussels, Rodin had made a copy of the famous Belvedere Torso as a symbol of the Arts, although it was signed with the name of his partner at the time, Antoine van Rasbourg. The example of the great ancient fragment may have encouraged him to accept this unfinished work as artistically complete, making it the first of his partial figures. In another collaborative project he had also made three bigger than life-size seated allegorical figures for a monument in Antwerp commemorating a former mayor named Loos. The *Seated Ugolino* thus comes out of a group of powerfully built seated figures that he had made after seeing related antique works as well as those of Michelangelo and Carpeaux.

When working on the final model for *The Gates of Hell* (Plate 18), Rodin envisaged including a *Seated Ugolino* at the lower right, opposite *Paolo and Francesca*. His many powerful drawings of the ill-fated father and his children are all posed with the parent seated, but the pose of this plaster sculpture does not accord with any in the drawings, which is not unusual, for Rodin did not make sculpture from drawings. He rejected the seated pose for *The Gates*, and this early sculpture sat in the artist's studio until it was shown in the exhibition of 1900. Photographs show that the original plaster lacked more than just the left leg, and it was propped up on two planks with another supporting the left elbow.

To the photograph of the *Ugolino* shown from its right side, Rodin pasted a sheet of paper that allowed him to make what is presumably a rough sketch of *The Gates of Hell*. We know that in its early stage he considered placing a sculpture of a seated Dante before the portal. (See the entry on *The Thinker*.) It is possible that he may have used this seated figure of *Ugolino* to visualize what such an arrangement might look like. An inscription in the artist's hand at the top of the attached paper appears to be the words, 'ira au pied de la porte' ['It will go at the foot of the portal']. I owe this reading to my colleague, Professor F. Barson of the Stanford French Department. The recurring ink lines above the plaster figure may have been Rodin's notations for the general organization of the sculptural groups he was making for the door. The two parallel lines to the left of the figure may have indicated that the portal was to be closer to the figure than the studio wall and door. We may see here how a photograph could stimulate the artist's imagination, particularly since the print shows the sculpture in front of the studio door that serves as a point of departure for the schematic drawing of *The Gates of Hell*.

The third photograph, taken in Rodin's exhibition pavilion of 1900, reveals that he had added a mound to support the figure. Among our 1977 discoveries in the Meudon Reserve was evidence that Rodin refused to abandon this figure. Some time between 1900 and his death he added to the body of Ugolino the head of a woman, one of the 'muses', who is shown planting a kiss on the forehead of the upright figure of *La Terre*. The group is half shrouded in a plaster-covered sheet, masking the absent left leg and forearm. The word 'Absolution' is written in pencil on the mound, but we cannot be sure it is in Rodin's handwriting or was put there on his instructions.

9–12. *St John the Baptist Preaching*. 1878. Plaster.

With this sculpture Rodin responded to the criticisms of ambiguity of meaning and of life-casting levelled against *The Age of Bronze*. He further strengthened his claims to being a statue-maker who could make an important public sculpture of a Biblical figure making a gesture that could be both rhetorical *and* symbolic. He seems to have been seeking to reinvigorate the tradition of religious figures by giving the *St John* greater credibility along with greater naturalness of attitude and psychological urgency. His work, however, grew out of Third Republic sculpture, which had become more serious in tone and naturalistic in modelling by comparison with that of the Second Empire.

From several points of view the figure seems in full stride, but from its right side, as seen in Plates 9 and 10, the forked stance is also credible as that of an orator, with both his feet firmly planted, his gestures enacting the prophecy of the Messiah's descent to earth from Heaven. Such a stance Rodin had seen, according to his own account, when an Abruzzi peasant named Pignatelli came to his studio looking for work as a model. Rodin tells us he

. . . undressed, mounted the model stand as if he had never posed; he planted himself, head up, torso straight, at the same time supported on his two legs, opened like a compass. The movement was so right, so determined, and so true, that I cried: 'But it's a walking man!' I immediately resolved to make what I had seen.

Rodin prefaced these comments by recalling, some thirty years after the incident, his first impression of the Italian:

I was seized with admiration: that rough, hairy man, expressing in his bearing and physical strength all the violence, but also the mystical character of his race. I thought immediately of a St John the Baptist; that is, a man of nature, a visionary, a believer, a forerunner come to announce one greater than himself.

Ruth Butler questions this account on the grounds that in the 1870s Rodin would still have followed the custom of conceiving first the subject for a major work. She cites Bartlett: 'Selecting the subject of "St John Preaching", he began a sketch half the size of what he intended the statue to be.'

Study for *St John the Baptist Preaching*. Plaster, half-lifesize, 1878. Meudon Reserve. Photo Bruno Jarret, 1979

Even when portraying a man in motion, Rodin did not succeed in allaying all doubt that he did not cast from life, as some Salon jurors reported to the government that Rodin probably took a *surmoulage* of parts of the body. One critic believed that 'M. Rodin exposes . . . the worst-built man in the world.' Another wrote, 'This Precursor recalls in no sense the legend of the great Apostle [sic], covered in goatskin, and preaching the coming of the Messiah. Give more liberty to

your timid imagination, M. Rodin.' Still another commented, 'For ugliness and triviality he approaches the extreme. M. Rodin shows us in his "St John" that vice has its manner of expression and ugliness its degrees. It would be difficult to find anything more repulsive than this statue.' The work was also praised as 'a marvel of reality, of intimate concentration, of a precise and significant execution'. Nevertheless, despite all the criticisms, the government honoured the sculpture by the purchase of a bronze in 1881. There were enlightened government officials who recognized the sculptor's genius and accepted such audacities as his break with traditional ways of showing the figure in movement:

> It was customary then, when looking over a model, to tell him to walk, that is, to make him carry the balance of the upright body on to a single leg; it was believed that thus one found movements that were more harmonious, more elegant, 'well turned out'. The very thought of balancing a figure on both legs seemed like a lack of taste, an outrage to tradition, almost a heresy. I was already wilful, stubborn, I thought only that it was absolutely necessary to make something good, for if I didn't translate my impression exactly as I had received it, my statue would be ridiculous. . . . I promised myself then to model it with all my might, and to come close to nature, which is to say, to truth.

The implications of 'balancing a figure on both legs' were explained by Rodin to Paul Gsell, when he discussed how the sculptor could rival not just the painter and dramatist but also the photographer. This explanation accounts for the difference between the *St John the Baptist* and Rustici's figure Rodin had seen in 1875.

> The sculptor compels . . . the spectators to follow the development of an act in an individual . . . the different parts of the figure represented at successive instants. They have the illusion of beholding the movement performed. . . . Have you ever attentively examined instantaneous photographs of a walking figure? . . . while my Saint John is represented with both feet on the ground, it is probable that an instantaneous photograph from a model making the same movement would show the back foot already raised and carried toward the other. Or else, on the contrary, the front foot would not yet be on the ground if the back leg occupied in the photograph the same position as my statue. Now it is exactly for that reason that this model photographed would present the odd appearance of a man suddenly stricken with paralysis and petrified in his pose. . . . If, in fact, in instantaneous photographs, the figures though taken while moving, seem suddenly fixed in mid-air, it is because, all parts of the body being reproduced exactly at the same twentieth and fortieth of a second, there is no progressive development of movement as there is in art.

Rodin's audacity with movement mingled with his desire to produce a finished sculpture by traditional standards. At this stage he was aiming for perfection, carrying his 'imitative art farthest'.

In Plate 9 we see that the figure was not yet fully realized in the relation of the feet to the base and in the absence of the right hand. Pignatelli posed for Henri Matisse in 1900 and told him how Rodin worked. Matisse believed the *St John* was a confusion of expression. He felt that expression should not be *depicted*, but should come from the artist and the total arrangement of the work. He 'could not understand how Rodin could work on his *St John* by cutting off the hand and holding it on a peg: he worked on the details holding it in his left hand . . . keeping it detached from the whole, then replacing it on the end of the arm; then he tried to find its direction in accord with his general movement.'

Rodin obviously worked on the plaster itself as well as working in clay from the model. (The pile of discarded material on the floor in Plate 10 could be plaster or clay.) Plate 10, whose overlayed graphite grid indicates Rodin used it for a drawing, helps us to see the changes made in the head, right hand, and the base. The photograph is not clear in the area of the extended right hand, so that it is hard to confirm that Rodin did not again change its position after the picture was taken.

The photographs showing the penultimate and finished *St John* (Plates 9, 10) reveal that the figure did not carry in his left hand a shepherd's cross, such as appears in a drawing Rodin did. The cross is drawn in a lighter tone than the figure, which suggests, as did the drawing of the plaster *Age of Bronze*, that Rodin may never have actually used a prop in either sculpture. If he had made a prop, quite probably he would have used photography, as well as drawing, to consider its effect in the ensemble. No such photograph has yet been found in the Musée Rodin archives. The sources of the *St John* are discussed in the entry on *The Walking Man* (Plates 132–4).

In the spring of 1977, I found in the Meudon Reserve a half life-size plaster version of the *St John*, possibly such as Cladel describes, one without arms but possessing completely finished and perfectly unified legs and torso, surmounted by an early study for the head. There are also two separate studies for the head. (These will be discussed and reproduced in a future study to be published as part of the proceedings of the 1979 International Congress of Art History in Bologna.)

Although it is not certain, it is possible that the second and even the first photograph (Plates 9 and 10) were made in Rodin's studio at 36 rue de Fourneaux (later rue de Vaugirard). The second two (Plates 11 and 12) may have been made in Rodin's government-owned studio in the Dépôt des Marbres at 172 rue de l'Université, as the last maquette for *The Gates of Hell* stands to the left of *St John*, and the sculptor was given this studio to carry out the commission for the great portal. In the photograph of *St John* from the back (Plate 12), one can make out in the lower left corner in clay or plaster the early state of *The Kiss* in which several limbs are missing. We do not yet know either the subject or the authorship of the small statue of a young man atop the corner cupboard in Plate 10 nor do we know the author of the graffito in Plate 11. (Rodin had assistants even in Belgium, when he was barely able to support himself and his family.)

13. *La Défense*. 1879. Enlarged version seen here *c.* 1899. Bronze.

Following the bitter defeat of France in the war against Prussia, the national government, as well as those of the various departments, commissioned monuments to the débâcle. They were intended to remind France of this humiliation and to contribute to the spirit of revenge against the Germans. In 1879, a competition was announced by the Préfecture de la Seine for a monument that would commemorate the defence of Paris. (Rodin had served for a few months in the national guard and was stationed in Paris, but saw no fighting.) The site chosen was the Rond-point de Courbevoie, since called the Rond-point de la Défense, which is on the north-west axis of the Arc de Triomphe and connected to it by the Avenue de Neuilly. The great relief on the Arc de Triomphe, *The Departure of the Volunteers of 1792*, was very much on Rodin's mind when he made his unsuccessful entry for the competition. Rude had symbolically shown Frenchmen of all ages responding to the call of the Spirit of Liberty to arm themselves and go into battle for their country. For his friend Paul Gsell, Rodin analysed 'this sublime war epic' as a 'true dramatic composition' in four phases, initiated by 'Liberty in a breastplate of brass, cleaving the air with unfolded wings,' who 'roars in a mighty voice "Aux armes, citoyens!" . . . Her mouth of stone shrieks as though to burst

Head of the wounded warrior in *La Défense*. Plaster, 1879. Meudon Reserve. Photo Bruno Jarret, 1979

your eardrum . . . no sooner has she given the call than you
see the warriors rush forward. . . .' Rodin's own conception is
like a tragic sequel to the departure of the volunteers, of which
now only one, mortally wounded, remains, supporting himself on a sword driven into the ground. In this figure, Rodin
used a Michelangelesque torsion, like that of Christ in the
Florentine *Pietà*, to effect a narrative that shows the one-eyed
warrior looking up or listening to the frenzied, disarmed, and
battered figure of Liberty, who in turn, is poised above a
cannon, whose mouth is driven into the ground. If Rude's
Liberty could deafen, Rodin's counterpart, played by Rose,
his mistress, could rally the dying from the grave. Just as did
Rude, Rodin sought to show that sculpture could 'compete
with the theatre'. Unfortunately, he could not convince or
move the jurors, who did not accord his entry even an honour-
able mention; the commission went to Barrias. Rodin later
expressed the view that in their eyes his work had 'too much
violence, too much vibration'.

14. The Trocadéro Fountain decorative masks. 1878. Stone.
Destroyed.

Bartlett tells us:

> Just before the great exhibition of 1878, Rodin was working
> for a certain decorative sculptor who was especially critical,
> and for whom he made a number of large heads, destined
> for the Trocadéro Palace, though eventually they were not
> used for that purpose. If they were not wholly satisfactory
> to the employer, he was yet quite willing to sign and exhibit
> them in the industrial art section of the exhibition, where
> they gained him a gold medal. In the same section, Rodin
> showed his 'Broken Nose' and some other works of like
> merit, but received no recompense. The heads were after-
> ward presented by their owner to the Trocadéro Museum,
> and are now regarded as prized examples, some say master-
> pieces, of modern French decorative sculpture, though no
> one knows who really made them.

Rodin's 'critical' employer was the sculptor Legrain, whom
Cladel referred to as 'Laouste'.

From this old photograph it is possible to see that, contrary
to Bartlett's statement, Rodin's decorative masks were, in
fact, used in conjunction with the fountain. It was at the base
of the great curved southern end of the Trocadéro Palace that
faced the Champ de Mars. The building had been designed
by Davioud and Bourdais for the 1878 exhibition. Rodin
provided the plaster models that were presumably stone-
carved by someone else. Grappe wrote: 'Having returned to
Paris and being unsure of what he would do next, he accepted
the offer to collaborate on the exterior decoration of the palais
du Trocadéro. These two mascarons in reduced proportions,
accompanied by a third, served as keystones on the arcades of
the monumental fountain.' The two masks Grappe refers to
are illustrated in his catalogue and are on the two arcades
flanking the centre arcade. The plasters for these masks have

Mascarons intended for the Trocadéro Fountain. Plaster, *c.* 1878.
Meudon Reserve. Photo Bruno Jarret, 1979

been in the Musée Rodin since 1927, when they were given by
the Museum of Decorative Arts. Both the plaster and the
stone of the central mask were reminiscent of the head of the
older Gaul who looks at his young companion in the centre of
the relief by Rude, *The Departure of the Volunteers*. This mask
seems to have been lost in both stone and plaster. Grappe
indicates that the stone versions were smaller, but this is hard
to verify from the photographs. I believe they were of the
same size, because they seem roughly three times the life-size
heads of the figure sculptures below them.

The mascarons have three different expressions: that on the
extreme left of the photograph, which bears a sea shell between its antlers, is smiling; the central one seems calm; and
the one at the far right is scowling. In a contemporary drawing
in *L'Art* of 1887, there is no indication that the flanking
mascarons were waterspouts, while the central one is blocked
from view by a cascade of water.

Although he does not mention the mascarons, in his 1889
guide to *Paris et ses environs*, Baedeker thus describes the
sculptural programme of the Trocadéro Palace, which housed
the museums of comparative sculpture and ethnography:

15. *Bellona*. 1878. Bronze.

This photograph of *Bellona* was made in 1900, during Rodin's one-man exhibition. The bust is displayed in the pavilion Rodin had specially built, and in the background is the plaster of *The Gates of Hell*, denuded of most of its figures. The date and original title, as well as Rodin's reasons for making this sculpture, are the subject of controversy. What is not in doubt is that his mistress, Rose, posed for it with a stern and thoughtful expression that Rodin told his biographer Cladel he had taken from life during one of their emotional 'scenes'.

Georges Grappe, one-time curator of the Musée Rodin, wrote in his still indispensable catalogue of 1944: 'Conceived decoratively, it was certainly finished by 1878, since at the beginning of the following year it figured in a competition for decorative art, but did not achieve success.' Grappe also wrote that this bust 'carried different names before that of Bellona. It was known as Clorinde, a sort of legendary Amazon who appears in Tasso's *Jerusalem Delivered*, Hippolytus, the young hero loved by Phaedra, and La République.' Truman Bartlett stated:

> In 1879, Rodin entered two competitions, one for a monument to commemorate the defence of Paris, and the other for a bust of the Republic. Neither was successful. . . . For the latter he made a large head wearing a helmet. Of it the journal *La France* said: 'A work of singular originality, but which the jury could not accept. Instead of a Republic, it represents a sullen Bellona with a physiognomy very dramatic.' On another occasion the same paper referred to the bust as 'a sculpturesque fantasy, a bedevilled fervour that makes one dream of Carpeaux when in his most audacious moments of imaginative composition.' Other notices of the bust did not fail to recognize that it was conceived from a different point of view from that which the public had been accustomed to seeing.

John Tancock rejects Grappe's date of 1878 on the assumption that Rodin made the work for the competition for a commemoration of the Republic that was not announced until 1879, and then he adds, 'It seems unlikely that Rodin would have tackled this subject on such a grand scale, solely for his own pleasure.' The scale is, in fact, life-size, and previously Rodin tackled entire life-size figures such as the *Ugolino*, *The Age of Bronze*, and *St John the Baptist* without commission and with the view to entering them in salons and presumably competitions. Busts of helmeted amazons were used in Rodin's day to symbolize variously victorious Gaul or civic virtues, as well as the Republic, as Tancock points out. We tend to forget that this world-renowned artist was first and always a French patriot, dedicated to serving his country and adding to the glory of French sculpture. He was aware of the demand by the government for patriotic themes, and *Bellona* was, in fact, purchased by the French government. Grappe is probably correct in his dating, and the variety of titles applied appropriately to this work would help explain why Rodin did not have to wait for a competition explicitly for the Republic.

From the lower basement there descends a monumental cascade, with jets of water that terminate in a basin surrounded by four animals cast in bronze: a bull, a horse, an elephant and a rhinoceros, by Caïn, Rouillard, Frémiet and Jacquemart. In the basin where the cascade falls, there are other animals of the same genre throwing off 'sheaves' of water, above all an elk strangled by a boa, a bear surprising a swan in its nest and two seals playing with a fish by Frémiet. Under the neighbouring arcades, *Water*, by Cavelier, and *Air* by Thomas. In the upper basin has been (tentatively) placed the model of a group showing La Seine and its two tributaries, L'Yonne et la Marne, by Falguière. On the balcony at each side: Europe, by Schoenewerk; Asia, by Falguière; Africa by Delaplanche; North America by Hiolle; South America, by A. Millet; Oceania, by M. Moreau.

Rodin's smiling mascaron is thus above Thomas's *Air*, and Cavalier's *Water* is below the frowning mascaron. Judging by Baedeker's account, the photograph of the fountain was taken after 1883, because of the presence of Falguière's 'model' of the Seine.

16. *Head of Rose*. 1880–2. Plaster.

In 1864, Rodin met a twenty-year-old seamstress, Rose Beuret, who became his mistress, the mother of his only son, his model, the caretaker of his works in clay and, finally, in 1917, a short time before her death, his wife. Rodin's portraits, such as the earlier *Mignon* and this one, show that Rose was a beautiful woman. That she was a person of strong character and great loyalty is confirmed by her history, for she endured almost twenty years of extreme poverty, during which time she helped support the household and suffered long separations from Rodin while he worked in different cities. This portrait mask, the last that he seems to have modelled as such from his mistress, was Rodin's favourite. Over the years it was redone in different media and in more amplified form as *L'Alsacienne*. The mask's quiet composure contrasts with the stern visage of *Bellona* and the screaming head of the spirit of Liberty in *La Défense*, which Rodin's biographies indicate were authentic expressions. Rodin was to comment that even in death his wife had a fine head for a sculpture. John Tancock properly dates this portrait 1880–1, based on a note on the back of a photograph of Rose formerly in the possession of Rodin's close friend and great biographer, Judith Cladel. (On the question of dating this work, see Mirolli, Grappe, Tancock and Spear.)

That Rodin chose to have a photograph made of a plaster still bearing the seams of its piece mould reminds us that presumably in the second half of the 1880s he began to exhibit works such as this that were by traditional standards unfinished. Photographs may have helped him study in a more detached way the effects of retaining marks of the sculptural process; they could have thereby influenced his acceptance of accident and chance in certain cases.

17. The third architectural model for *The Gates of Hell*. 1880. Plaster, 105 × 60 cm.

Made in 1880, this last model of the portal mediates between preliminary drawings that showed a series of panels in low relief and the final, more three-dimensional conception with its dramatic range of reliefs and full figures. As Rodin moved from drawing into modelling, he was inspired to break with tradition and develop his own conception in theme and form. The placement of the seated forms of Paolo and Francesca at the lower left, next to the seated Ugolino with a dying child on the lower right, indicates that he was following neither Dante's narrative sequence nor his construction of Hell. The pose of the Ugolino in the model differs from the freestanding plaster in that the father is more upright and holds a dying child on his lap. To date it has not been possible to identify any of the other figures with specific characters in *The Inferno*. The seated figure at the top, which we know as *The Thinker*, may have been Dante, meditating on his poem. The muscular quality of this small figure echoes the ample-bodied figures discernible below, while Rodin's drawings of Dante invariably stress his fragile frame and bearing. What seems prophetic in the model, besides the location of *The Thinker*, is

Rodin's effort to integrate the architecture and sculpture into a total decorative effect, rather than to have the architecture play a passive role.

18. *The Gates of Hell*. 1880–1917. Plaster.

The project that led to Rodin's full realization of his powers as a sculptor and which caused him to crystallize his personal way of working was *The Gates of Hell*. Commissioned by the French government in 1880, they remained in plaster and not finished to his complete satisfaction at his death in 1917. Most of the work on this project appears to have been done within the first six years, for the artist indicated to the government at that time that he could deliver a finished work. The Museum of Decorative Arts, for which it was intended, was not built on the projected site, now the Gare d'Orsay. When the present museum was installed in 1900 as an extension of the Louvre it was in a new building, the Pavilion Marsan, on the Rue de Rivoli. According to Rodin, the architect was not anxious to have the portal; hence it remained in his studio. *The Gates* were not cast in bronze until 1928.

Although it could not have been foreseen by Edmond Turguet, the French Minister of Fine Arts, one of the greatest sculptural projects in history resulted from his confidence in a relatively unknown forty-year-old sculptor, who had been accused of life-casting his two publicly exhibited statues. Rodin accepted the challenge to vindicate himself. In view of the widespread interest in Dante among nineteenth-century sculptors and painters, the choice of subject was not surprising. It is not absolutely certain whether Turguet or Rodin established the theme, but in all probability it was the artist:

I had no idea of interpreting Dante, though I was glad to accept the *Inferno* as a starting point, because I wished to do something in small, nude figures. I had been accused of using casts from nature in the execution of my work, and I made the *St John* to refute this, but it only partially succeeded. To prove completely that I could model from life as well as other sculptors, I determined, simple as I was, to make the sculpture on the door of figures smaller than life. My sole idea is simply one of colour and effect. There is no intention of classification or method of subject, no scheme of illustration or intended moral purpose. I followed my imagination, my own sense of arrangement, movement and composition. It has been from the beginning, and will be to the end, simply and solely a matter of personal pleasure. Dante is more profound and has more fire than I have been able to represent. He is a literary sculptor. He speaks in gestures as well as in words; is precise and comprehensive not only in sentiment and idea, but in the movement of the body. I have always admired Dante, and have read him a great deal, but it is very difficult for me to express in words just what I think of him, or have done on the door. . . . The salient subjects of the door are the two episodes of Paolo and Francesca da Rimini and Ugolino, but the composition includes three phantoms and Dante. . . .

Although he exhibited many plaster figures from the portal before 1900, this photograph shows its first public appearance as a whole. The entire preceding year, at great expense, Rodin had a large group of assistants at work finishing and assembling the entire portal. For the move from his government studio in rue de l'Université, he probably disassembled the figures, as the portal was re-erected in at least two horizontal sections minus the figures in high relief. Once it was installed, it seems that he chose not to have the full complement of sculptures exhibited. Precious evidence of dissatisfaction with his own work are his handwritten notes on the photograph: '*Moins grosses de dimensions/ Les mouleurs plus incolorés, plus fines.*' After viewing the depleted portal Rodin judged that the dimensions should be less bulky and the mouldings less colourful and more fine. This accords with his objectives of achieving a new decorative unity between sculpture and architecture.

19–24. *The Thinker*. 1880. Clay.

Talking to a critic and friend, Marcel Adam, Rodin said in 1904:

> *The Thinker* has a story. In the days long gone by, I conceived the idea of 'The Gates of Hell'. Before the door, seated on a rock, Dante thinking of the plan of his poem. Behind him, Ugolino, Francesca, Paolo and all the characters of *The Divine Comedy*. This project was not realized. Thin, ascetic, Dante separated from the whole would have been without meaning. Guided by my first inspiration, I conceived another thinker, a naked man, seated upon a rock, his feet drawn under him, his fist against his teeth, he dreams. The fertile thought slowly elaborating itself within his brain. He is no longer dreamer, he is creator.

Rodin's photograph of the early *Seated Ugolino* (Plate 7), to which he added what was probably a schematic sketch of *The Gates*, may have been an attempt to visualize what a figure seated in front of the portal might have looked like. The *Seated Ugolino* now seems to us another important source of *The Thinker*. Invaluable photographs of *The Thinker* in clay show it in its original scale with its armature visible between the feet. In the third and last architectural sketch for the portal, Rodin had already decided to change the pose, so that the right arm crosses to the left knee and the left forearm lies along the left thigh. In the final work he rotated the gesture of the torso inward to the left, thus setting up a contrast with the splayed position of the legs and a series of torsions in the figure that added drama to the passive pose. As discussed in the entry on *Ugolino*, *The Thinker* has a rich ancestry within both Rodin's art and art that preceded his conception, including the *Ugolino* of Carpeaux, the work of Michelangelo, and the Belvedere Torso.

In Plate 19 we see that Rodin has brought the figure almost to completion. Comparison with a second photograph of *The Thinker* in clay (Plate 20) seems to indicate that some touches of untempered clay had been removed from the figure's left

side, just above the creases made by the torso's position. In the second photograph we can see, however, that in the chest area Rodin has kept some small rough slabs of clay that he seems to have applied over pectoral areas previously modelled. By this thickening of form was Rodin making intuitive judgements based on his anticipation of how the whole would look from a distance, eschewing the more consistent finish sustained in the *John the Baptist*?

Rodin's drawn notations in Plate 19 may have constituted directions to the photographer or to himself to animate the sculpture or increase value contrasts on these surfaces. Since he has drawn over the forehead, it is hard to tell. In this photograph we may be seeing his way of editing by cutting into an area (note the cuts by the figure's left elbow and upper arm), creating a flaw or breach in a previously finished surface, as a way of re-entering the completed modelling, anticipating greater depressions in contrast to the added touches.

Despite its pedestrian appearance, what is exciting to scholars about Plate 19 is the sight of the plain board armature in the background. This is the first time we have seen what in all probability is the wooden framework to which Rodin added clay as he built *The Gates of Hell* in 1880. (In the background of Plate 48, we can see the clay mouldings of the lower portion of the portal.) The wooden planking indicates Rodin had conceived of recessed panels above a large moulding. The vertical boards indicate the width of one of the two vertical panels on which so many figures would be placed. In Plates 21 and 22, Rodin has mounted the clay figure of *The Thinker* on a scaffolding in order to study it from below. Just where it was to go, however, may not have been decided upon, as the lintel area seems to have been too shallow at this stage. In the last clay model, Plate 17, *The Thinker* is not set within the lintel, but is positioned in front of a vertical divider that bisects the space behind him. In an earlier architectural drawing Rodin had conceived of placing the figure of *Eve* in the centre of the doorway, like a medieval figure of the Virgin before a Gothic cathedral portal. This may have been in his mind when these photographs were taken. In the upper part of the photographs we can see that the wooden armature is curved or pitched upward at the top, and this feature was to be drastically changed.

It has been argued that what we see in these early photographs was Rodin's image of Dante. Ruth Mirolli adheres to this opinion largely on the grounds of the quotation already given and the fact that from at least 1885, writers who visited Rodin's studio referred to this figure as Dante. It was not Rodin's custom to correct interpretations by his visitors, and he seems to have assented to a plurality of readings of many of his figures. Whether this was out of tact, respect for the writer's imagination, or recognition of the variety of meanings in his figures, we cannot say for sure. We do not know if the writers confirmed their interpretations with Rodin or how often they were influenced by what others had written before them. Rodin was probably ambivalent about the identity of the figure from the start. First of all, his drawings of *The Divine Comedy* earlier than and contemporary with the inception of *The Gates* frequently show Dante as a slender, fragile figure. His statement to Marcel Adam indicates that even in 1904, he recalled his vision of Dante as thin and aescetic. Rodin had a sense of old-fashioned artistic decorum that was part of his conservatism. His own later explanation that he conceived 'another thinker' is entirely congruous. In 1889, he exhibited at the Galerie Georges Petit this figure with the title: *The Thinker: The poet, fragment of a door*. At some point *The Thinker* came to represent the artist and is a spiritual self-portrait of its creator. Rodin believed in a fraternity of creators which gave equality to poets and sculptors, and 'poet' was a title with which, as a sculptor, he felt comfortable.

Studying the gum bichromate print in Plate 24 against a regular one from the same negative reminds us of Rodin's response to Baudelaire's criticism of sculpture that it is susceptible to being seen from viewpoints unintended by the artist and that 'often it is humiliating for the artist when a chance ray of light or illumination from a lamp uncovers a beauty which the artist had not intended.' To Edmond Claris, Rodin wrote,

> It is not correct to say that a chance light . . . can discover a beauty which did not occur to the artist, since a 'well made' work of art contains all the forms necessary to render the expression and the movement of life which animate the subject. It is therefore impossible, no matter what the lighting, to find a form that has not been willed.

Dépôt des Marbres help us to understand Rodin's interest in showing this figure in as lifelike a way as possible. Though inspired by Michelangelo's *Eve*, Rodin's fallen woman looks natural in the shadows of the same studio where the model, Madame Abruzzezzi, had posed for her many years before. Rodin recalled to Dujardin-Beaumetz his reactions to this beautiful woman when he first saw and modelled her:

> The dark one had sunburned skin, warm, with the bronze reflections of the women of sunny lands; her movements were quick and feline, with the lissomness and grace of a panther; all the strength and splendour of muscular beauty, and that perfect equilibrium, that simplicity of bearing which makes great gesture. At that time I was working on my statue 'Eve'. Without knowing why, I saw my model changing. I modified my contours, naively following the successive transformations of ever-amplifying forms. One day, I learned that she was pregnant; then I understood. The contours of the belly had hardly changed; but you can see with what sincerity I copied nature in looking at the muscles of the loins and sides. It certainly hadn't occurred to me to take a pregnant woman as my model for Eve; an accident – happy for me – gave her to me, and it added the character of the figure singularly. But soon, becoming more sensitive, my model found the studio too cold; she came less frequently, then not at all. That is why my 'Eve' is unfinished.

25–26. *Eve*. 1881. Bronze.

Rilke described *Eve*'s gesture of withdrawal into the self:

> . . . it shrivels like burning paper, it becomes stronger, more concentrated, more animated. That Eve [which] was originally to be placed over *The Gates of Hell*, stands with head sunk deeply into the shadow of the arms that draw together over the breast like those of a freezing woman. The back is rounded, the nape of the neck almost horizontal. She bends forward as though listening over her own body in which an alien future begins to stir.

At the outset of his project, Rodin intended to position life-sized statues of Adam and Eve on either side of *The Gates of Hell*. *The Gates* were not bronze cast in Rodin's lifetime, and this arrangement was only carried out a few years ago by the Musée Rodin in its garden. Rodin's interest in doing several statues based on Biblical themes in the late 1870s and 1880s coincided with their frequency in the sculpture salons of these years. (Scholars refer to this as religious genre art, as it was not commissioned by the Church.) Rodin did not show *Eve* to the public in bronze until 1899, in which year this figure was displayed with its base buried in the sandy floor of the exhibition hall. Such an audacious installation drew the comment that Rodin was a revolutionary.

Druet's daring photographs of *Eve* in the studio at the

27–28. *Ugolino and His Sons*. 1880–1(?). Clay.

Dante's story of the Pisan count, imprisoned with his sons and grandsons for betraying his native city, was the earliest of the themes in the *Divine Comedy* to be interpreted by Rodin. The *Seated Ugolino*, Plate 6, dates from 1877 at the latest. Many drawings witness Rodin's attraction to, if not obsession with, this theme of cannibalistic infanticide. The two clay versions reproduced in Plates 27 and 28 were probably photographed in 1880 or 1881, with the naked wooden armature of *The Gates* behind one of them. Rodin has dramatically altered the *mise-en-scène* of the theme from that of the seated pose in the third architectural model. He was probably inspired by a rereading of Dante and the lines describing the last days of the ill-fated family left to starve in a dungeon:

> When we had come to the fourth day, Gaddo threw himself stretched out at my feet, saying: 'My father! Why don't you help me?' There he died; and even as thou seest me, saw I the three fall one by one, between the fifth day and the sixth; whence I betook me, already blind, to groping over each, and for three days called them, after they were dead; then fasting had more power than grief.'

It is not impossible that the kneeling figure of Ugolino started out in a seated posture, as suggested by viewing these photographs as if they were in a vertical format. The earlier of the two shows Rodin's dissatisfaction with the top of Ugolino's head; and he subsequently changed the whole head, lowering its position and eliminating the details of the bared teeth. He also changed the pose of the child who lies directly under Ugolino. In the form found in *The Gates*, he has returned to the boy's original posture with the head down. The version of *The Gates* shows the group from the side opposite to that revealed by these photographs, indicating that Rodin had no fixed viewpoint from which to see the figures when he was working on them for the portal.

Rodin's revision of the staging of the Ugolino theme to a horizontal format was later accompanied by a similar transformation of his Paolo and Francesca group. These alterations may have been prompted by his changing views of the portal and a desire to have less static or self-enclosed motifs and to allow the damned to partake more of the space around them. *The Gates*, as they evolved, did not have a predetermined space, one established by an ideal observer outside the portal; and each figure and group that was inserted created its own ambience, so that in the final portal Ugolino and his sons are shown on the ground, while below them Paolo and Francesca seem to soar in space. Like Dante voyaging through the Inferno, *The Gates* seem composed with a roving focus.

From contemporary sources it is clear Rodin used Pignatelli, who had posed for the *John the Baptist*, as the model for *Ugolino*. It is interesting to see how literal or 'realistic' was Rodin's interpretation of the dying count. His stomach is contracted both from fasting and from the effort of crying out. The earlier *Seated Ugolino* was far more thick-waisted.

29. *Ugolino and his Sons*. After 1889. Plaster.
Meudon Reserve.

A third distinct version of the Ugolino theme that I found in the Meudon Reserve in the spring of 1977 shows a composite of the moribund infants from the second version, clinging to or lying across the lap of their father. It is thus closer to Rodin's drawings of this theme from the 1870s. Ugolino's head has been changed and is that of the male figure used for '*I Am Beautiful*' and *Avarice and Luxury* and is not that of the second Ugolino. Further, the body is arguably that of a woman, the seated *Cybele*, for which Madame Abruzzezzi posed in 1889, which is when Grappe dates the first small version of this work. This figure was shown headless, the right hand addressed to the right shoulder, and the knees together. Rodin on several occasions created bisexual figures, notably in what is probably a very late assemblage titled *Absolution*, in which the first torso of the Ugolino is surmounted by the head of a woman, that of *Eurydice* used for a muse and Eurydice in *Orpheus Imploring the Gods*. Except for the grafting of the head to the body of the parent, this group today shows the most rudimentary joining. It survives in a highly fragile state, but is precious testimony to Rodin's audacities with composition and his use of his plasters as readymades available like a repertorial group for new encounters.

30. '*I Am Beautiful*' ('*Je Suis Belle*'). 1882. Plaster.

Known variously in the artist's lifetime, according to Grappe, as *The Kiss, The Rape, Carnal Love,* and *The Cat,* this couple, which derives from *The Gates of Hell,* bears the present title because of Baudelaire's verse inscribed on the base of a later cast:

> *Je suis belle, ô Mortels, Comme un rêve de pierre*
> *Et mon sein, où Chacun s'est meurtri tour à tour*
> *Est fait pour inspirer au poëte un Amour,*
> *Étant alors muet ainsi que la matière.*

(In the poem 'La Beauté', the last line reads *Éternel et muet ainsi que la matière.*) This sculpture appears in the upper right bas-relief of *The Gates.* The man's back is turned toward the viewer so that the woman can hardly be seen. In addition, the male figure, for which Pignatelli was supposed to have modelled, appears in the portal as a falling man and as one who is clutching another woman just above the tomb in the right panel in a grouping entitled *Avarice and Luxury.* The female figure from '*I Am Beautiful*' appears almost behind *The Thinker* in the lintel of *The Gates* and was shown separately as *The Crouching Woman.*

Affinities of modelling rather than psychological interchange between figures justified such chance couplings, according to the artist, but estrangement between intimately paired figures is an important motif in Rodin's epic of humanity's fate. The passionate acrobatics of this couple remind us of how much he depended not just on his models, but on surprising possibilities afforded by his own art. As remarked in the introduction, the ink drawing suggests that Rodin had planned to increase the amplitude of the base to counterbalance the unclassical massing of the sculpture at the top.

31. *The Crouching Woman*. 1880–1. Clay.

When Rodin determined to make *The Gates of Hell* by following his own imagination with 'no scheme of illustration', it appears that he set out to make a large number of expressive figures without a clear idea of where they would be located in the portal. As a case in point, *The Crouching Woman,* by all accounts, was one of his first figures, yet in *The Gates,* besides being shown in the upper right relief ('*I Am Beautiful*'), she is located almost behind *The Thinker* in the lintel, an area Rodin seems to have worked on later than the side reliefs and two central panels.

In this earliest revision of the motif the woman's gesture of grasping her left foot in her right hand compositionally completes the self-enclosure of the figure and also recalls the French idiom for orgasm as putting one's foot in one's hand. The pose of the body is unprecedently compacted, and together with the gesture of her left hand, which squeezes her breast, it suggests giving birth and nursing a child, as if Rodin was evoking the woman's dream of having a child or her lament for a lost one. (Elsewhere in the portal there are children without parents.) No more powerful single figure exists in sculpture to express a narrative of unrequited love.

32–33. Fugitive Love. 1881(?) Before 1887. Clay(?) Plaster(?).

'When the figures are well modelled, they approach one another and group themselves by themselves.' When Rodin told this to Dujardin-Beaumetz, he added, 'I copied two figures separately; I brought them together; that sufficed, and these two bodies united made Francesca da Rimini and Paolo.' Rodin could have also been speaking about the work made many years before known as *Fugitive Love*. According to Grappe, it was originally titled *Night and Dawn* and later *The Dream, The Way to the Abyss* and *The Sphinx*. (Grappe mentions a Rodin inscription on an old photograph, 'Voici venir . . .,' which is the beginning of a verse by Baudelaire.) The male figure of *Fugitive Love* is also the *Prodigal Son* or *Child of the Century* that Rodin used by itself as well as in *The Gates of Hell* and which, because of the pose of the uplifted arms, could have derived from the apparently lost 1870s sculpture of Joshua imploring the sun to stop in its course.

While from the photograph it is difficult to tell whether the composition is in clay or plaster, it is quite possibly in the former, as there are still rough areas in the man's chest, the sharp cutting in the base suggests clay, and the couple seem to have been attached to a base by its use. The ladder visible in one of the photographs may have been the one used for work on *The Gates of Hell*, and judging by the scale of the piece in relation to the studio keys near it, Rodin may have had the actual clay version for *The Gates* photographed. In one photograph the sculpture of *Fugitive Love* is tilted upward, so that the photographer could obtain more light on the woman and still another angle from which the artist could study the recent marriage of the forms. Within *The Gates of Hell*, all orientations were possible, and Rodin was to be more venturesome in floating or disposing his figures in his sculpture than in his drawings, where they are more consistently seen in contact with the ground.

Grappe tentatively dates this group before 1887, but it is not impossible that they were done at the beginning of the decade, during the explosive years of creativity that brought the portal near completion in 1884, at which time Rodin had a foundryman estimate their cost. (The weight of the bronze cast then, as now, was to be eight tons.)

34–35. Fallen Caryatid Carrying her Stone. 1881. Bronze.

Rilke has described the *Fallen Caryatid*:

A woman's form kneels crouching, as though bent by the burden, the weight of which sinks with a continuous pressure into all the figure's limbs. Upon every smallest part of this body the whole stone lies like the insistence of a will that is greater, older and more powerful, a pressure which it is the fate of this body to continue to endure. The figure bears its burden as we bear the impossible dreams from which we can find no escape.

The caryatid, intended for *The Gates of Hell*, may have come out of Rodin's thoughts, conveyed in the third architectural

model (Plate 17), for expressive single figures along the portal's sides. The model's more titanic figures recall those of Michelangelo and reflect Rodin's struggle to absorb that artist's ideas. Shortly after he began work on *The Gates*, however, he gave up his ideas of working from Dante and also from Michelangelo; he turned to working directly from the model, putting nature before his eyes. It was this crucial decision to work obstinately from life, to take his postures from those unselfconsciously assumed by men and women who posed for him, that finally and irrevocably separated him from Michelangelo. Because his models were not professionals, trained to assume art poses, and because he watched their movement at all times, including moments of rest, his study helped him to broaden the body language of sculpture.

Within *The Gates*, the *Fallen Caryatid* occupies the upper left corner and is largely concealed from the spectator's view from below by a heavy drapery. As we can see in the photograph of *Despair* (Plate 94), Rodin was at times given to masking his figures partially with a blanket or drapery, as if they were seen in a cave, accentuating their mood of withdrawal. The gum-bichromate print further solicits different interpretations of the figure by muting its details and its environment. It was characteristic of Rodin to realize a beautiful and expressive form completely and then spend a lifetime obscuring or working against our experience of the original totality. Whether or not the pencilled darkening of the drapery and left leg of the figure were notations for the photographer or to himself to reconceive or block out this area, we do not know. This is one of Rodin's more symbolic figures and rare in the use of an object as part of the motif. In other versions the caryatid carries an urn. It could have inspired Georges Minne's later kneeling adolescent stone-bearers.

36. The Shade. Enlarged in 1898. Plaster.

Shortly after his return from Italy in 1875, Rodin is supposed to have worked on a sculpture of Adam, directly inspired by having seen Michelangelo's art, especially his *Adam* on the Sistine Ceiling. Dissatisfied with what he had done in his inquiry into Michelangelo's methods, Rodin reportedly destroyed the first version and did a second, which exists today and was intended to flank *The Gates of Hell* along with a statue of Eve. He made a different or third version of the figure, which came to be known as *The Shade*, changing the left arm with its pronated gesture for one pointing downward and away. Its original scale was about one-third life-size, and three identical casts of this figure, minus their hands, were placed atop *The Gates of Hell* some time in the early 1880s. Rodin referred to this group as 'the Phantoms', when he spoke of the Dantesque motifs remaining in *The Gates* after he had decided to personalize the project. The inspiration for putting the three figures on top of the portal may have come from Rustici's group of three figures on top of one of the doors to the Florentine Baptistery. Rustici's *John the Baptist*, the central figure in the group, had been a point of departure for Rodin's own figure of that name. In 1898, Rodin's assistant who specialized in enlarging and reducing the master's work, Henri Lebossé, made the enlargement of *The Shade*. In his beautiful photograph, Bulloz shows the life-size plaster probably outside Rodin's Meudon studio. This photograph reminds us that Rodin liked to test the resistance of his modelled planes to disintegration under strong sunlight. By focusing on the great back, Bulloz recalls the observation of Rodin's contemporaries that he had a 'democratic style', which meant not just avoiding a false Greek idealism, but also giving the entire figure an equal expressiveness. From Judith Cladel we know that the original model was a circus strong man named Caillou, who worked in Paris fairs and on the streets and who could lift 100 kilos with his teeth. Rodin liked this powerful athlete, for as a model he was 'soft as a rag'. What helped to win critics to his art early in his public career were figures such as this that demonstrated 'solid anatomical knowledge'; and in Bartlett's words, 'The artist who shows such a hardy work must really have, as they say, "something in his stomach".'

37. See note to Plate 39.

38. *Meditation* or *The Inner Voice*. 1885 or 1896–7. Plaster.

This figural fragment, edited by the artist, represents but one state of many, discussed in detail by John Tancock, since the figure's first appearance in the extreme right of the lintel of *The Gates of Hell*. What we see in the photograph is probably the original scale, roughly thirty inches, of the sculpture that Rodin had enlarged to sixty inches, a cast of which was given to the Musée des Beaux-Arts in Marseilles in 1898. The Meudon Reserve has casts of the smaller, original version. It was Rodin's practice to have several plasters cast of the same figure so that he could rework the limbs, for example, while retaining the original. The amputations in the area of the legs probably relate to his addition of drapery when the figure was being considered as one of the muses in the monument to Victor Hugo. Rodin placed the arms in differing positions, and in the original *Meditation*, the left hand presses the left breast in a way reminiscent of the gesture of *The Crouching Woman*. Their co-existence in the lintel of *The Gates* enhances their spiritual, if not thematic, affinities.

The fragment we see is already an assemblage of the legs from *Eve* joined with a torso that exemplifies Rodin's love of torsion or what he called 'désinvolture'. The joining of the lowered head with the shoulder evokes the sense of the woman's inner listening. The energy of the pose is thus generated not from external causes, but in response to an inner condition. Rodin explained to Paul Gsell the fragmented state of this dynamic ruin by saying: 'My figure represents Meditation. That's why it has neither arms to act nor legs to walk. Haven't you noticed that reflection, when persisted in, suggests so many plausible arguments for opposite decisions that it ends in inertia?' Rilke describes this sculpture:

Never was a human body assembled to such an extent about its inner self, so bent by its own soul and yet upheld by the elastic strength of its own blood. . . . It is striking the arms are lacking. Rodin must have considered these arms as too facile a solution of his task, as something that did not belong to that body which desired to be enwrapped within itself.

39. *The Shade with Meditation*. After 1898. Plaster.

37. *The Shade with the Fallen Caryatid*. After 1898. Plaster.

These sculptures vividly display Rodin's use of inconsistency in mode and scale within a single composition. He developed a strong personal sense of what could constitute the intrinsic character of sculpture; and that character could be violated only, in Rilke's words, by:

the movement that does not complete itself within the thing, that is not kept in balance by other movements. . . . he knew that that which gave distinction to a plastic work of art was its complete self-absorption. It must not demand or expect aught from outside; it should refer to nothing that lies beyond it, see nothing that is not within itself; its environment must lie within its own boundaries.

The closed eyes, symptom of an almost total withdrawal into the self, and their act of touching give the figures this quality of self-absorption. The photographer, guided by Rodin, helps us to see how the sculptor viewed the movements of the paired figures as completing themselves.

The Shade with Meditation was acquired by the Ny Carlsberg Museum, revealing Rodin's interest in releasing one of his most venturesome 'études' to a public collection. The present location of *The Shade with the Fallen Caryatid* is not known to the author. While all of the figures date from the early 1880s, the enlargement of *The Shade* was made in 1898. The photograph was presumably taken in the Hôtel Biron, into which Rodin moved in 1908. There is at present no way of knowing, however, when the pairings were made.

40. *The Martyr*. 1885. Plaster.

41–42. *The Martyr* or *The Broken Lily*. 1911. Marble.

43. *Icarus*. 1895(?) Marble.

44. Enlarged torso of *The Martyr*. 1898(?) Plaster.

Within the lintel of *The Gates of Hell*, the figure later known as *The Martyr* appears immediately behind *The Crouching Woman* and to the left of *The Thinker*. In her original upright position she is shown running. (The figure was attached to *The Crouching Woman*, as it could not stand by itself.) Rodin chose to show her separated from the portal, as if having fallen on her back: hence the title *The Martyr*. Also, within *The Gates*, she appears, largely draped, as a fallen angel who lies on top of the tomb at the portal's lower left. Her right arm extends downwards, and in her hand she holds a wheel, perhaps symbolizing Fortune. This particular area of *The Gates* was a late change, and the inclusion of the fallen angel may have been inspired by the figure of *The Martyr* having been used for marble sculptures of *Icarus* (Plate 43) and *The Broken Lily*. The latter was a commission for his own tomb by Marius Sourisseau, who died in 1907, and the carving was installed in the Saint-Acheul cemetery at Amiens in 1911. Rodin chose to have a series of photographs made of the process by which *The Broken Lily* came into being.

The first photograph shows an armature propping up the figure, which outside *The Gates* literally could not stand on its own. (Study of this photograph may have influenced Rodin's subsequent decisions.) The general outline of the draped armature prefigures the shape of the subsequent stone background. The second photograph shows how the form had been roughed out by the *metteur au point*. The stone bears graphite indications of additions and changes that Rodin wanted, notably more articulation of the thorax and sternum, the addition of wings and the lengthening of the left leg. The third photograph shows the relief completed by a *practicien*. Carved on the marble are the words by Alfred de Musset, 'Dieu passe, il m'appelle.' These pictures allow us to see the changes, approved by Rodin, made by his carvers in the proportions, detail and surface of the plaster.

Sourisseau may have been influenced in his commission by having seen the marble *Icarus*, the plaster of which dates from 1895, and the marble was photographed by Druet some time after 1898. Not only was this figure susceptible to additions or changes in the position of the head and arms, but it was subdivisible. One of the most beautiful photographs ever taken of a Rodin sculpture is that of the torso of *The Martyr*. (Given the marble *Kiss* at the left, the photograph may date from 1898.) What we see is probably its enlargement by Henri Lebossé, who would present Rodin with parts of figures in clay as he finished with them. Their casting in plaster by a Rodin assistant certified the master's approval. (To my knowledge there is no bronze casting of just the torso, and what we see in the photograph probably became a full figure of *The Martyr* or the *Half-length Figure of a Woman*.) The presence of the camera tripod at the right and the rolled newspapers on the lap of the male figure in *The Kiss* does not detract from the composition of the whole. They help make us aware of the sculpture's existence, not as a precious object, but as a part of a workshop, where we see it in transit, not to a customer, but to a new existence. One could imagine Rodin's instructions to the photographer as being what he told Dujardin-Beaumetz: 'We never see anything in isolation; an object is always in rapport with what is in front, beside, behind, above, below. The relations are important.'

45. *Madame Alfred Roll*. 1882 or 1883. Plaster and clay.

One of the most beautiful portraits of a woman done by Rodin in marble is that of the first wife of the painter Alfred Roll. The marble dates from 1884, and this plaster probably predates it by at least a year. Grappe indicates that the marble was intended for the triennial Salon of 1883, but was not ready in time. The delay may have been due to Rodin's *practicien*, who

did the delicate carving, as Grappe indicates; but as this photograph shows, it was the sculptor's custom to put aside a plaster for a period of time in order to study it and, as in this case, perhaps add something, such as the clay flowers which appear in the marble. In this work the mode of modelling that contrasts the firmness of the flesh with the looser touches of the costume recalls Carpeaux's modelling and reminds us of Rodin's exposure to the Second Empire style and its ideal of femininity. The variable focus and spirited sculptural notations of the hair and costume are replaced in the final marble by a more consistent definition. Despite her humble situation here, in a photograph that was probably intended only as a proof, the woman's poise and the expressiveness of her glance are undisturbed. Rilke had reservations about portraits such as this and wrote about the portrait of Mme Vicuña:

> This portrait survives partly because of a certain graciousness which has been hereditary for centuries in French plastic art. It shines somewhat with the elegance of the inferior sculptures of French tradition; it is not quite free from that gallant conception of the 'belle femme' beyond which the serious and the deeply penetrating work of Rodin grew so quickly. One should remember that he had to overcome the ancestral conception, had to suppress an inborn capacity for this flowing grace in order to begin his work quite simply. He must not cease to be a Frenchman.

46. *Antonin Proust*. 1884. Clay or bronze.

From a time shortly after the Paris exhibition of his *Age of Bronze* until his death, Rodin had the friendship and support of many French government officials connected with the arts, such as Antonin Proust. They helped with government purchases of his work and sent many important visitors and clients to his studios. In turn, Rodin often gave works of art, plasters, prints, and occasionally a bronze, to friends who had helped him, and he often did their portraits, as in this case. This beautiful finished photograph by Bulloz is possibly of a raw bronze (*font brut*) with its casting seams still unchased and one of the sprues, or bronze channels, still in place, protruding from the head. More likely, we are looking at an *estampage*, a clay impression taken from a piece mould of the original clay portrait. The protruding 'pipe' may be the internal armature. That Bulloz and not Bodmer photographed it suggests this was done many years later, in the late 1890s. Rodin would take clay impressions in order to effect changes, while preserving the original as a reference. The bistre tinting of the photograph makes it difficult to distinguish with certainty the material of the bust. The plaster armature at the base permits the argument that Rodin was expanding the bust and wanted internal support until moulds were made for recasting.

The simple upright pose of the head accords with the politician's aristocratic features. The latter dictated Rodin's modelling. Such portraits first won Rodin universal acclaim as a great artist, and many clients saw their immortality as residing in his hands. Looking at this bust, one is reminded of his comment to Dujardin-Beaumetz:

A beautiful bust shows the model in his moral and physical reality, tells his secret thoughts, sounds the innermost recesses of his soul, his greatness, his weaknesses; all the masks fall off. It is a resurrection, for one feels the souls of his ancestors revive in him. Through his own sensibility, the artist becomes a revealer, a diviner.

47. Auguste Rodin in 1880.

This photograph shows Rodin at the time he began *The Gates of Hell* and was working on the sculptures reproduced on the preceding pages. The plaster-splattered clothing evokes his profession and self-image as a worker, a man who suffered for, married and was saved by his art. The pose of folded arms, prophetic of a later study for his monument to Balzac, conveys for sculptor and writer the sense of a man who could do anything, rather than passivity. In a rare recorded self-analysis, Rodin said, 'I have a rather heavy and sad temperament. I am not a dreamer, but a mathematician'.

48. *Eternal Spring*. 1881(?) Clay.

Rodin produced a small group of embracing figures in the early 1880s, including *The Kiss* and *Eternal Idol*, which may have been destined for *The Gates* but did not receive tenure. Bodmer's photograph shows *Eternal Spring*, first titled *Zephyr and the Earth*, in clay form, and behind it may well be the lower section of *The Gates*, also still in clay. The way that the male figure overlaps the base suggests the couple were destined for the portal. As it became apparent to Rodin that his epic would be tragic, themes that evoked a joyful exercise of the passions were probably removed. The lovers within *The Gates* are shown despairing or pulling away from each other.

Instead of portraying his figures as deities or symbolic attributes, Rodin democratized the embrace and choreographed it in passionate abandon. That he did so has been attributed to his practice of having models move freely about the studio. *Eternal Spring*, however, is not a chance encounter of models left to their own devices. The body of the woman comes from the *Torso of Adèle* that Rodin had first made in Nice while working there in 1879. *Eternal Spring* is a work not of observation but of imagination, an assault on thematic taboos and compositional restraint. The photograph of this sculpture in clay permits us to re-experience the freshness of the modelling before it became neutralized by Barbedienne's commercial reproductions.

49. *The Helmet-Maker's Wife* or *The Old Courtesan*. 1880–3. Bronze.

50. *Triumphant Youth*. 1894. Plaster.

Earlier and alternative titles for *The Helmet-Maker's Wife* were *The Old Woman*, *Winter*, and *The Old Courtesan*. Rather than an illustration of François Villon's poem, 'Celle Qui Fut La Belle Heaulmière', Rodin's stunning depiction of age was made directly from an old model who had previously posed

for his assistant, Jules Desbois. Caira sat for reliefs on a ceramic vase and for *The Gates of Hell* in the early 1880s, as well as for this study of a self-contemplating crone, whose right hand, extended behind her back, belies the submissive pose, as seen from the front. To make the image even more lifelike, Druet photographed the bronze by artificial light, using a sodium ring and reflectors, and from certain close-up angles that caused a peripheral blurring which suggests optical distortion.

The acquisition of this sculpture by the State and its placing in the Palais de Luxembourg was an act of confidence and courage, as there was public protest against its 'ugliness'. Brought to his attention by Paul Gsell, this criticism inspired Rodin's discourse:

The vulgar readily imagine that what they consider ugly in existence is not a fit subject for the artist. They would like to forbid us to represent what displeases and offends them in nature. It is a great error on their part. What is commonly called *ugliness* in nature can in art become full of great beauty . . .

Rodin then cites precedents in older art and literature of great artists transfiguring the 'ugly', and he goes on to say:

In fact, in art, only that which has character is beautiful. Character is the essential truth of any natural object, whether ugly or beautiful . . . it is the soul, feelings, the ideas expressed by the features of a face, by the gestures and actions of a human being. . . . Now to the great artist, everything in nature has character. . . . And that which is considered ugly in nature often presents more character than that which is termed beautiful . . . in all deformity, in all decay, the inner truth shines forth more clearly than in features that are regular and healthy. . . . Whatever is false, whatever is artificial, whatever seeks to be pretty rather than expressive, whatever is capricious and affected, whatever smiles without motive, bends or struts without cause, is mannered without reason; all that is without soul and without truth; all that is only a parody of beauty and grace; all, in short, that lies, is ugliness in art.

According to Grappe, in 1894 Rodin added the drapery and figure of an adolescent girl, creating a composition which was variously titled *The Grandmother's Kiss* and *Fate and the Convalescent*. He also introduced behind the sculpture an open pair of scissors that now seemed to have fallen from the old woman's outstretched hand, as if she had been cutting cloth across her knees when interrupted by the impetuous embrace of the young girl. Such a narrative or anecdotal device is rare in Rodin, recalling the book held by Paolo in *The Kiss*. Perhaps by means of a clay *estampillage*, Rodin inclined the old woman's body without otherwise changing the modelling, as her head is pulled downward to that of the girl. The paradox is that the solitary figure of the old woman was seen by Rodin's contemporaries as literary, which it was not, whereas its later version is actually more evocative of a drama, ambiguous as its meaning might be. Paul Gsell reminded

Rodin that, while he was admired by 'literary people', his 'censors' blamed him for having an 'inspiration more literary than plastic', to which he replied:

> If my modelling is bad . . . if I make faults in anatomy, if I misinterpret movement . . ., the critics are right a hundred times. But if my figures are correct and full of life, with what can they reproach me? What right have they to forbid me to add meaning to form? How can they complain if, over and above technique, I offer them ideas?

One is permitted to think that more than chance dictated the photographing of the plaster cast of *Triumphant Youth* in the courtyard of Rodin's studio in the Dépôt des Marbres against a background of 'ruins'.

51–64. *The Burghers of Calais.* 1884–9.

If we had been with Bracquemond and Edmond de Goncourt on Saturday afternoon, 17 April 1886, when they visited Rodin's studio on the boulevard de Vaugirard, we probably would have seen what these photographs show us. In de Goncourt's words, 'Rodin turned on their saddles [sculpture stands] the life-size clay figures of the Calais hostages, modelled with a powerful accusatory realism and the beautiful holes in the human flesh that Barye put in the flanks of his animals.'

Two years before, perhaps because he felt he was close to finishing *The Gates of Hell*, Rodin had submitted a model which won him a commission from the city of Calais in which he was:

> to execute and carry through to completion . . . the composition and the plaster model of the group of Eustache de St Pierre and his companions, which is to include six figures . . . no less than two meters average height. . . . The model of the group must be completely finished and carefully executed, in the same manner as the works submitted to the annual salons. . . . Beforehand . . . M. Rodin will make . . . a plaster model one-third the final size of the monument, thoroughly worked out, finished and completed, needing only to be enlarged and perfected. He will, however, ultimately incorporate in the final group any changes the committee would suggest on examination of said model.

Rodin contracted to deliver the final figures in plaster by 1885, which he failed to do, even taking on other projects such as the abortive monument to Vicuña-McKenna, a model of which is shown in Plate 72.

Unlike his method in *The Gates of Hell*, Rodin followed the story given in his commission. The circumstances leading to the commission, ably researched by Mary Jo McNamara, involved the desire of Calais not only to show its patriotism and win prestige with a modern monument, but also to symbolize the old city of Calais that was about to be merged with the adjacent city of St-Pierre. Rodin's monument was to be part of the modernizing of the rejuvenated port and in-

dustrial city, and by a wonderful historical irony, England was to build a tunnel connecting Dover to Calais. It was the successful attempt by England in the fourteenth century to gain a foothold on the Continent at Calais during the Hundred Years War that led to the siege of that city and the sacrifice of the Burghers of Calais. After a long siege, and against the opposition of his knights, King Edward III succeeded in imposing a brutal peace by asking for the lives of the six leading citizens of Calais, terms contrary to the rules of war. Froissart's *Chronicle*, written many years later, recounts the story of the six successively rising in a town meeting to offer their lives; stripping to their shirts and breeches and putting on halters in the market-place; being led through the city gate with the keys to the city; arriving at the English camp to confront the king and his executioner; and then being spared at the intercession of the pregnant queen. In the eighteenth century, largely through the writing of Voltaire, the oldest burgher, Eustache de St Pierre, was accused of being a traitor. Despite subsequent rebuttals, it fell to Rodin to proclaim once and for all the citizens' belief in Eustache and to celebrate his devotion. Rodin persuaded his client to agree to a monument

Eustache de St Pierre. Bronze, on exhibition alone at the Paris Salon. Photographer unknown, salt print, 26 × 20 cm (cat. no. 1464)

to all six, and he chose the fateful moment of departure rather than the scene at the English camp customarily favoured by painters. Politically, the figure of Eustace was the most important in the group, and Rodin took the greatest pains with it, even in the photographs.

Until these old photographs were discovered in the spring of 1977, we did not know in what arrangement the second model, prescribed by the contract, disposed the figures. The model can be seen in the background of Plates 55 and 56, behind the naked figure designated Pierre de Wiessant by a former director of the Musée Rodin. (In Rodin's lifetime only two figures seem to have been assigned names, Eustache de St Pierre and Jean d'Aire.) This uncertainty arose because Rodin chose to make the figures for the second model separately and to experiment with them in various combinations.

One cannot be absolutely certain that what one sees in the photograph was the arrangement Rodin showed the Calais commissioners, as the photographs do not show if the bases of the figures were connected. A description in *La Patriote* of 2 August 1885, places the figure with the keys at the extreme right on the other side of Eustache de St Pierre.

Pictures of four of the Burghers still in clay show the great detail with which they were reworked; Rodin had contracted to produce sculptures of a finish equal to that in the salons. As with the *John the Baptist*, he worried over the positioning of feet and hands, frequently changing them. 'The expressions of the personalities are arrived at by the correct modelling of nuances,' was his comment. Like the most conservative academic sculptor, he realized his figures first in the nude and then applied a form of surplice, rather than shirts and breeches. The 'accusatory realism' observed by de Goncourt, Rodin saw as work 'prepared sincerely and not for a charming effect'. His monument was crucial in the fight against 'the outmoded sculptural style' and false 'theatrical art' of the École des Beaux-Arts. Rodin's interpretation of the story had a strong moral basis, for, as he told Gsell, 'The more frightful my representation of them, the more people should praise me for knowing how to show the truth of history.'

Not until 1889 did Rodin finish and exhibit all six of the burghers in plaster. He rejected one of the figures in his second model, the second from the left, and at the time of these photographs two may have remained to be done. A variety of setbacks postponed the inauguration of *The Burghers* until 1895, when against Rodin's wishes they were installed not where he had intended but next to a public lavatory in front of a park, mounted on a pedestal and set off by a fence. At all stages of the monument's making, it was criticized for its unheroic, irreverent, and even vulgar figures, for its lack of both style and conventional pyramidal composition, and for a certain monotony due to the even line of the heads within a cubic configuration.

In every way Rodin sought to be original in *The Burghers*. To Paul Gsell he recounted his intentions:

I have not shown them grouped in a triumphant apotheosis; such a glorification of their heroism would not have corresponded to anything real. On the contrary, I have, as it were, threaded them one behind the other, because in the indecision of the last inner combat which ensues between their cause and their fear of dying, each of them is isolated in front of his conscience. They are still questioning themselves to know if they have the strength to accomplish the supreme sacrifice – their soul pushes them onward, but their feet refuse to walk. They drag themseves along painfully, as much because of the feebleness to which famine has reduced them as because of the terrifying nature of the sacrifice. . . . If I have succeeded in showing how much the body, weakened by the most cruel sufferings, still holds on to life, how much power it still has over the spirit that is consumed with bravery, I congratulate myself on not having remained beneath the noble theme I have dealt with. I did not want a pedestal for these figures. I wanted them to be . . . affixed to the paving stones in front of the Hôtel de Ville in Calais so that it looked as if they were leaving in order to go to the enemy camp. In this way they would have been mixed with the daily life of the town.

The gum bichromate prints permit us to see, as Rodin would have us see, how the figures compose and recompose themselves as we move about them. This movement should be in counter-clockwise fashion, as if we were standing still and they were walking past us. Rilke, who perhaps of all Rodin's contemporary interpreters, understood his intentions best, writes of *The Burghers* in a way which helps us to understand why Rodin would have admired these gum prints:

Besides the points of actual contact there is a kind of contact produced by the surrounding atmosphere which diminishes, influences and changes the character of the group. . . . To Rodin the participation of the atmosphere in the composition has always been of greatest importance. . . . When interpreting nature he found, as he intensified expression, that, at the same time, he enhanced the relationship of the atmosphere to his work to such a degree that the surrounding air seemed to give more life, more passion . . . to the embraced surfaces.

65–70. *The Clenched Hand* or *The Expressive Hand*. 1885(?) Bronze.

Rilke, who knew Rodin's work intimately, wrote in 1903:

There are among the works of Rodin hands, single small hands which without belonging to a body, are alive. Hands that rise, irritated and in wrath; hands whose five bristling fingers seem to bark like the five jaws of a dog of Hell. Hands that walk, sleeping hands, and hands that are awakened; criminal hands, tainted with hereditary disease; and hands that are tired and will do no more, and have lain down in some corner like sick animals that know no one can help them.

Rodin's preoccupation with hands may have begun when he was taught to model sculpture at the Petite École in the mid-

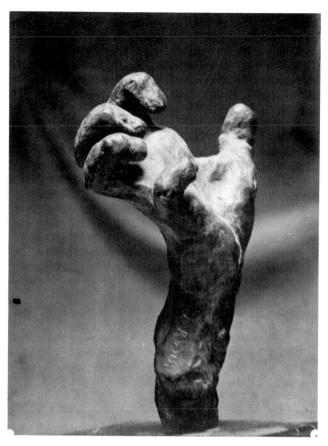

The Clenched Hand. Bronze, 1885? Photo Druet, gelatin silver print, 39.8 × 30 cm (cat. no. 1484)

1850s by working first from parts of figures. This was also a practice at the École des Beaux-Arts, for which the Petite École was a preparatory school. Photographs show us that Rodin paid the greatest attention to the hands of his life-size figures, such as the *John the Baptist* and *The Burghers of Calais.* It is possible that this particular hand, as well as a comparable treatment of the left hand, may have been destined for one of *The Burghers of Calais,* but was not used because it did not accord with the feeling of the whole figure. It is just as likely that Rodin made the hand with no figure in mind. The project for *The Gates of Hell* unquestionably encouraged the sculptor's study of all possible expressions of which the hand was capable. These works were admired by poets such as Rilke and Verlaine. Aaron Scharf has suggested that Rodin might have been motivated to exhibit the hands by themselves as a result of studying Muybridge's photographs of hands in *Animal Locomotion,* and John Tancock sees an influence from Victor Hugo's drawing of an upraised hand emerging from a sleeve and titled *The Dream.* Five views of Rodin's bronze hand with its base masked by a blanket were published over the title *Expressive Hand* in the special issue of *La Plume* devoted to the artist's work in 1900. (The side view we illustrate was not included.) There is a half-size study for

this hand, and, in addition, Rodin combined its enlarged version with the upper half of the *Centauress* in one of his fantasies evoked not by literature but by his art itself.

71. *Faun and Satyr.* 1886. Clay (terracotta in the Rodin Museum).

The Rodin Museum possesses this work in terracotta, but it is not recorded in Grappe. It seems not to have been bronze cast. The presence of the legs of one of *The Burghers of Calais* in the background at the upper left of this photograph helps to date this work, for Rodin worked on several projects at once. That the sculpture was made in the rue de Vaugirard studio rather than the Dépôt des Marbres suggests that it was not intended for *The Gates.* The mythological motif recalls Rodin's Second Empire upbringing as an artist and his life-long delight in the art of Clodion and the eighteenth century. (Academicians were more tolerant of lusty themes if they involved satyrs and fauns.) Even when he modelled such 'modern' amorous couples as *The Kiss* and *Eternal Spring,* Rodin did not reject mythological motifs. He was always an artist who kept his options open and refused to turn his back on the past.

There exists in the Meudon Reserve a marvellous plaster figure without head or arms, but kneeling and twisting at the waist in the same manner as the faun in this sculpture.

72. Model for a *Monument to Benjamin Vicuña-McKenna.* 1886. Clay (apparently lost).

In 1886, Rodin received a commission for a monument to a Chilean statesman and historian, Benjamin Vicuña-McKenna. It was probably through his friendship with the Chilean ambassador and his wife, Madame Luisa Lynch de Morla Vicuña, of whom he had earlier made a beautiful marble portrait, that Rodin was asked to do not only this monument but one of General Lynch. Neither monument was ever realized, and only the equestrian model for the Lynch project has survived. In this photograph, probably taken in 1886, in the same studio where Rodin was working on *The Burghers of Calais,* we can see for the first time the clay model of the monument, on top of which stands Vicuña-McKenna, holding a flag. Below, the personification of Chile or Fame looks up to him, presumably in admiration. There were to be three bas-reliefs; and that on the front below the personification was to show a scene in the Chilean Parliament.

Just how extensively Rodin's assistants would work on such a project is indicated by a bill in the Musée Rodin archives dated 22 September 1886, for the services of Abel Poulin, a childhood friend who worked for a time as an assistant. In his account of services, Poulin writes of working on the architecture which was scaled at 10 centimetres to the metre. He also specifies considerable reworking, adjusting and joining ornament consisting of three laurel garlands and two groups of laurel leaves falling downward on the lateral faces of the monument; adjusting the three bas-reliefs and work on architectural ornament such as capitals for the pilasters at the corners; careful adjustment, positioning and joining of the personification on the front and of trophies of arms on the back; engraving of an inscription above the personification, and so on. A literal translation of the bill is difficult because of what appears to be a special use of the noun '*trainage*', which normally means pulling behind, dragging or trailing, as with a sled, and the verb '*trainer*', which means to drag along or out, to pull or to draw. Since Rodin made a rough sketch for the monument, which is also in the Musée Rodin archives, and gave instructions to Poulin, we are here taking these words to mean not that Poulin hauled the maquette or its parts to Rodin's studio, but carried out his instructions by executing and redoing various parts of the model.

The details of Poulin's bill and a frontal view of the model taken at the same time, which is in the Musée Rodin photographic archives, suggest that he may have done more work on the model after the pictures were taken. We know that Rodin redrew the profile of Vicuña-McKenna and the flag over one of the photographs. The photographs do not show the inscriptions, and the architectural details were far from being worked out. Poulin's bill was for 420 francs, and since the wage for a skilled worker, such as he, was 1 franc an hour, he must have worked more than 400 hours or seven 60-hour weeks on the project. From Poulin's accounting, it would seem that Rodin occupied himself with the overall conception, but actually modelled only the figure of the statesman with the flag and the personification. Such a division of labour was customary in Rodin's day.

In 1891, Rodin wrote to tell the head of the committee for the monument that casting in bronze would cost 79,900 francs, but that transport costs were additional. By 1901, the 85,000 francs had not yet been subscribed in Chile, and the project seems to have been dropped by mutual consent.

73–75. The *Monument to Claude Lorrain*. Begun 1884, inaugurated 1892.

In 1884, Rodin won not only the competition for *The Burghers of Calais*, but also one for a project proposed by the city of Nancy to commemorate the painter Claude Lorrain. In his winning application that accompanied the model, Rodin wrote:

The preoccupation in this project has been to personify, in the most tangible manner possible, the genius of the painter of light by means of a composition in harmony with the Louis XV style of the capital of Lorraine. In Claude Lorrain's face surrounded with air and light, it is proposed to express the painter's attentive admiration for the scenery amidst which he stands. The idea is that the statue itself should be in bronze, the socle with its decorative group, in stone.

Also quoted by Frederick Lawton in his 1908 book on Rodin is the sculptor's reading of the finished work:

My Claude Lorrain has found, and is admiring what he always found, what he always admired, and what we find and admire in his pictures – a splendid sunrise. The broad orange light bathes his face, intoxicates his heart, provokes his hand armed with a palette, so that the good workman may be recognized in him. The resemblance I caught in this way. The best and only likeness I have of him is just Marchal's face, the painter Marchal. This is a happy chance for me and flattering to Marchal. So I have a living Claude Lorrain, instead of a sheet of paper more or less covered with black strokes. As regards the soul, the thought, the genius of Claude, I had his pictures, in which he has put the sun, and himself.

In Lawton's own words:

The decorative group was an exceedingly beautiful representation of the Apollo myth. Beneath the entablature the Sun-God and his horses issue from the rocky mass of the shaft that typifies night and gloom. Only the forequarters of the animals and the upper body and head of Apollo are visible. Black clouds envelop and hide the rest. One hand the god raises to thrust the whelming darkness from him; and with the other, he guides the onward rushing steeds.

In response to the criticism of having left the hindquarters of the horses in the clouds, Rodin actually had them recarved, to his later regret. He did nothing about the accusations that the socle outshone the statue and that the painter was too human seen against the god. His drawing on the photographs shows a greater concern with his realization of the painter's face and the profiling of the base where it met the statue.

Rodin was able to take on several major commissions at once because he had excellent professional sculptors working with him. Freuler's beautiful salt prints on the thinnest of paper, suggesting a date in the 1880s, show the big wooden shed in Nancy in which the final sculpture was prepared. The shed provided not only a protected space, but as the photographs show, good light with and against which to study the parts and the whole.

76. *President Sarmiento*. 1894–6. Bronze.

Photographed outside one of Rodin's studios, the bronze statue of Domingo Faustino Sarmiento may have been awaiting transport to Argentina, where it was unveiled in 1900. The distinguished founder of public education in his country had died in 1888, and Rodin built his rugged likeness from photographs that showed the late president seated in formal attire. Without his usual recourse to studies of a naked figure, Rodin had built the form in a series of half-size studies showing the educator clothed, standing in a somewhat exaggerated hip-shot pose. At the same time he was working on his monument to Balzac, which showed the great writer standing, deep in thought, and wearing a bathrobe. One of the final additions to the Sarmiento figure was the cape thrown over the topcoat, winding around the figure and curling in front of the left leg, thereby augmenting the contrast of rest and movement by which Rodin sought to dramatize an essentially stationary subject. Photographs of preliminary models show that he used stiff paper in studying how to give the form greater amplitude; and the final cape does have the look of coming from such a source rather than from actual cloth like that he was draping over his Balzac studies. Rodin gave the head of this man of letters far greater force by means of a more powerful cranial structure than photographs suggested; and in this change the artist may have been guided by descriptions provided by Sarmiento's friends.

In the final monument the bronze statue surmounts a marble pedestal, decorated with an allegory that the commissioners requested. For this, in Lawton's words:

> He combined the Apollo and Hercules myths, and modelled a god in high relief on a background of cloud and shadow, the god extending his arms to cast the darkness from him, while one hand crushed a snake, and his feet spurned other venomous creatures that crawled below. This tableau represents Sarmiento's fight with ignorance and his victory over its opposition.

77. *The Metamorphoses of Ovid*. Before 1886. Plaster.

This couple is found in the upper right corner of *The Gates of Hell* in an upright position, as seen in this photograph, but turned so as to produce a view showing the back of the kneeling woman embracing her recumbent companion. There is a version without a base reproduced in Grappe, the figures upright, as if one woman sits across the knees of her kneeling lover. The later marble version shows the couple in the prone position in which the artist arranged the plaster. The pencil notations on the photograph suggest possible reworking in the upright pose, perhaps for the marble. Thus, we see Rodin visualizing the work not only in a horizontal position, but vertical, free-standing, on a base, and against a cliff. The models for this sculpture were lesbians from the Paris Opera. Its title was once *Gemini*, and in another photograph, not reproduced, Rodin drew the arc of a circle across the bottom, as if to suggest the zodiac title.

78. *The Juggler* or *The Acrobat*. 1892–5. Bronze.

Grappe lists the plaster for this work as being from 1909, but acknowledges that it must probably date from the early 1890s. He further attributes the subject to Rodin's interest in the circus and the improvised dances of the Montmartre night world. At one time the work was called *Triton and Nereid*, and in 1903 Rilke referred to it as *The Acrobat*. Both figures were modelled separately and led independent lives apart from their juxtaposition in *The Juggler*. In the Meudon Reserve there are enlargements of the woman, seated and grasping both feet in her hands; while the male figure is once shown upright, straddling the shoulders of a standing woman who had served as one of the symbolic figures of *Night* and *Day* for

the *Tower of Labour*. Rodin's use of the crouching woman in '*I Am Beautiful*' demonstrates that no pose is so self-sufficient that he could not conceive of it in union with another. Rilke pointed out that what is crucial in Rodin's compositions are the points of contact between the figures and whether or not their gestures complete themselves within the imaginary orbit of the sculpture itself. The photograph shows what appears to be a heavily 'antiqued' bronze, whose whereabouts today is not known, but which was characteristic of certain finishes Rodin preferred after 1900.

79. *Couple Seen from the Back*. Date unknown, possibly 1890s. Plaster. Whereabouts unknown.

This plaster may relate to the 'poet and Siren' idea, of which a marble was made around 1900. The seated figure was probably Rodin's *Seated Man*, who recurs in a number of small compositions, as well as by himself. The woman curving behind his head is a hybrid of a seated feminine torso to which Rodin added arms to enact a gesture without regard to scale, proportion, accuracy of bone and sinew in the shoulders, or to consistency of mode. The base shows the addition of liquid plaster over previously dried plaster, as if he wanted to counter the weight at the top through the augmented base. An outstanding example of Rodin's improvised couplings, this small sculpture evokes his ideas about composition based not on psychological or anecdotal affinities but rather the mutual attraction of well-modelled *morceaux*. He commented to Dujardin-Beaumetz: 'A composition is only beautiful in so far as it is the exact expression of what the artist intended to communicate. What has this composition, this expression of nature, in common with those rules of convention where one is taught to group personages in a certain order?'

80. *A Night in May*. Date unknown. Plaster(?). Whereabouts unknown.

The title is that of a poem by Alfred de Musset, to whom Rodin also dedicated a beautiful stone relief, *The Poet and His Muse*, before 1905. The flying figure, into whose head Rodin stuck pins to evoke a halo, was a favoured one the artist used severally, sometimes changing the head as well as the axis of the flight. Such abandon in couplings sometimes led him to suggest not only dreams of love, but also the artist and his inspiration, which to him were interchangeable themes.

81–82. *Young Girl Kissed by a Phantom*. 1880s(?). Plaster(?).

Writing about many of Rodin's paired figures is comparable to listing the stage appearances of an actor or actresses in a programme. For example, the recumbent woman in this sculpture appears in *The Dream* before 1889 (Grappe 237), and as a winged figure who hovers above a woman reclining face downward, who in turn comes from *The Gates of Hell*. The woman kissed by a phantom later appears in a solo performance in the Salon of 1896 as *Illusion, Daughter of*

Icarus, and in the artist's one-man show of 1900, playing the role of *Fallen Icarus*. The phantom seems from the waist down to be materializing from a cloud, but the torso and the pose of the arm over the head are found in comparable reclining male figures. Rodin's graphic notations indicate that he thought about introducing greater contrast and definition to the figures, adding legs to the phantom and perhaps wings to the woman. In addition, he saw this couple as upright caryatids for some future architectural decoration. A marble was carved of this motif around 1900, according to Professor Daniel Rosenfeld of Boston University.

83–84. *Twilight and Dawn*. Date unknown, male figure 1882. Plaster. Whereabouts unknown.

To read Rodin's words, his injunctions to follow nature obstinately, leaves one unprepared for so many compositions that even the most acrobatic and double-jointed models could not assume. In the white plaster world of his devising, Rodin arrogated to himself the making and breaking of laws and rules in order to formulate his own dreams. What kept work and art fresh was his experience of fortuitous couplings that revealed 'unexpected shades of feeling'.

The diving male figure in Plate 83 comes from *The Gates of Hell*. It bore the title of *The Despairing Adolescent*, according to Grappe, who dates it 1882, and may have been descended from Rodin's now lost figure of *Joshua* of the 1870s. His replacement in Plate 84 is less easily identifiable. The woman in both sculptures resembles the terracotta figure in the National Gallery of Art in Washington of *Eve Eating the Apple*, which may also date from the early 1880s.

85–88. *Victor Hugo*. 1883. Clay.

Dujardin-Beaumetz records the following account by Rodin:

The first time I saw Victor Hugo, he made a profound impression on me; his eye was magnificent; he seemed terrible to me; he was probably under the influence of anger or a quarrel, for his natural expression was much more that of a good man.

I thought I had seen a French Jupiter; when I knew him better he seemed more like Hercules than Jupiter. He had been so solicited for his portrait or his bust that he didn't want to pose; furthermore he had just given long hours to a sculptor named Vilain. Victor Hugo believed that after David d'Angers . . . no one would be capable of doing his bust. Madame Drouet arranged that he pose for me for half an hour, but that was all. He was so convinced that I was going to make a bad bust that he wouldn't even look at it. . . . I worked entire hours in the veranda of the hotel filled with flowers and green plants. I saw Victor Hugo sometimes, across the salon, hard and cold of aspect; he would also go and sit at the end of the room, absorbed, reflective.

The director of the Petite École, Lecoq de Boisbaudran,

made me follow a method which has . . . the advantage of being possible – I learned to draw a great deal from memory and thus I learned to observe; this always proved useful to me, but especially here, in this case.

You know that I hold as a principle the comparison of all the contours of a work with those of nature. Being unable to follow my habitual procedure, I placed myself beside or behind him, following him with my eye, making quick sketches of him, drawing as many profiles as I could on little squares of paper; he didn't look at me, but had the goodness not to dismiss me; he tolerated me. I made many drawings of the skull; then I compared those contours with those of the bust; thus I managed to execute it, but with such difficulties . . . I believe I rendered the first impression I felt. I worked three months, then I was given to understand that the bust was finished. I took it away.

Taking into account the background, these photographs seem to have been taken while the clay bust remained on the closed veranda of Hugo's home near or at the end of the four months Rodin worked on it. It may be Rodin himself who is visible in one of them. A letter to William E. Henley, written by Rodin before Hugo's death and six months after the portrait was 'finished', indicates a longer time period that that given in Rodin's later account quoted above. Lawton quotes Rodin as saying in the letter to Henley:

He has not – what is called – posed. But I have lived with him, lunching, or driving, or frequenting his soirées for the last four months, with the bust at his house, which allowed me to work there always. Sometimes I was with him whole afternoons, but I did not have him as a model that one places as is most convenient for the purpose.

89. *Monument to Victor Hugo in the Palais Royal (Victor Hugo and the Muses)*. 1897. Plaster.

This was the penultimate of many versions of Rodin's projected monument destined for the Palais Royal. The final marble version was of the writer seated alone, arm extended, 'silencing the noises of the world'. The public was dismayed at the sight of the exiled writer half-naked and, as described by Rodin, 'sitting on the Guernsey rock beaten by the waves'. The three inspiring muses of earlier versions had been reduced to two, *The Tragic Muse*, seen on the rock above the pensive poet, and *The Inner Voice*, behind him and not visible in this photograph. Notes from Lebossé to Rodin when the enlargement was finished reflect the sculptor's concern about the gap between Hugo's left arm and shoulder. Despite the enlarger's assurance it would be closed, Rodin chose to exhibit publicly in the Salon de la Société Nationale a conception that even if perfectly finished would have been controversial. There is also a gaping hole in the left arm of *The Tragic Muse*, and the armature of the big plaster is clearly visible, along with the iron support for Hugo's left hand. In his writings Rodin comments that even when anatomical possibility is violated, the requirements of a gesture for the composition, such as that for *The Tragic Muse*, come first. When he exhibited her by herself, Rodin at times preferred to show her in the enlarged version without the left arm.

90. Study for the *Monument to Victor Hugo* in the Panthéon. 1897(?). Plaster.

Rodin never achieved his planned monument to Victor Hugo destined for the Panthéon, but from it came this extraordinary study of an over-ripe 'Hercules', as Rodin often referred to Hugo. The photograph was probably taken of the enlargement to life-size from a smaller model. It was Henri Lebossé's practice to enlarge portions of the figure, submit them for Rodin's approval, and then join them in the studio after they had been plaster-cast. Lebossé was at work in the autumn of 1901 on the enlargement of a naked figure of Victor Hugo. The final figure was to be garbed, but Rodin, who had watched Hugo pace through his home, found a vigorous model of the right age and proportions to help him build the final statue from the inside out. As with *The Walking Man*, both feet are flat on the ground, but the upper torso is less erect, as the sculptor planned to show the writer meditating, thereby conjoining the active and contemplative.

91. *The Tragic Muse*. Before 1885. Plaster.

92. *The Tragic Muse and a Son of Ugolino*. After 1906. Plaster.

In his pavilion Rodin showed *The Tragic Muse* detached from the maquette for the Hugo monument. (Grappe dates the marble version 1885.) One of his most expressive and despairing heads had been joined to the neck of the kneeling form. In Plate 92 Rodin has united with the Muse the fragmented torso of one of Ugolino's sons, which in that group bears the head of *Sorrow* and is the figure grasping at his father's back. As the figure of the son was enlarged by Lebossé by 1906, the pairing of these figures must be later. Turning the seated figure upright gave the body a totally different expression. Rodin may have been inspired to effect this unlikely union of figures not just by the compatibility of the modelling in both figures, but by the way the overall gestures of the respective bodies complemented and contrasted with each other. Their amazing, somewhat oval arabesque in depth is compounded by strenuous rotations of the limbs at every flexible joint. No two comparable limbs of these united figures move in the same axis! Rodin's capacity to break loose from traditional norms for uniting figures on the basis of narrative or mutuality, such as was seen in *The Kiss*, resulted from an audacity of vision that pushed his art further into abstraction of form without loss of his subject's humanity. Photography was a precious device to record inspired but impermanent unions that he probably would have referred to as his *études*.

93–94. *Despair*. 1890. Bronze.

This figure appears in *The Gates of Hell* and thereafter in different sizes and materials. In the basement at Meudon are

versions stripped down to the torso alone, as if Rodin planned to attach other heads, legs and arms. Grappe, who dates the work in 1890, suggests that the model may have been an acrobat. The date is probably much earlier, and the model may have been seen by the artist simply stretching her back after a long session, for the pose does not require gymnastic prowess. The French idiom that equates putting one's foot in one's hand with sexual orgasm may have occurred to Rodin and made this unusual and expressive pose all the more appropriate for *The Gates of Hell*, where a small version of the sculpture is found.

Rodin had this figure carved in stone, and the bronze we see may have been made from a plaster prepared for that purpose. Masking part of the figure situates it in a cave-like ambiance, a technique Rodin used in some of his illustrations for Baudelaire's *Fleurs du Mal*, and it also fragments the figure, focusing our attention entirely upon the contracted and extended limbs. The daring photograph of the figure in foreshortening stresses the compactness of the form, while again serving to make it seem fragmented by throwing the projecting leg out of focus. Reversibility was instinctive to Rodin, who looked at a fragment in terms of possible additions and at a complete figure as susceptible to subtraction.

95. *Iris, Messenger of the Gods*. 1891. Bronze.

96. *The Crouching Woman* (with the head of *Iris*). *c.* 1913(?). Plaster.

Only in recent years have works such as these been exhibited with frequency and written about with enthusiasm by scholars and artists. According to Grappe, a winged version of *Iris, Messenger of the Gods* was once intended to surmount the project for a seated *Victor Hugo and the Muses*, suggesting that Glory crowned his efforts. It was thought a cancan dancer modelled for this figure. The earliest study has a head, but in versions subsequent to that shown in Plate 95, Rodin eliminated the head and also cut away the left leg, except for the upper thigh. Given the pose of the figure, it would have been impossible for Rodin to have practised his method of profile modelling. The original small version, like its enlargement, shows only rudimentary planar construction of the back. It is possible that Rodin modelled most of it from memory and in great haste to fix the figure's flight; or else he had the model stand erect, supported on one foot, to sustain the pose longer and then treated the left leg as if she were in the air. Rodin's breach of tact in exposing the sexual organs of the woman undoubtedly inhibited his showing the work in public for some years. By 1914, when he made his donation of fourteen sculptures to the Victoria and Albert Museum, he had a secure reputation and many partisans in England. As part of that donation, he included a bronze cast titled *The Crouching Woman*, for which he conjoined enlargements of the body and head from at least two different models and sculptures.

97–98. *The Kneeling Faun.* Before 1884. Plaster.

99. *Orpheus and the Furies.* 1884(?) Plaster.

In a pose that recalls Rodin's observation of the natural movements of his models, his *Kneeling Faun* is photographed in what was probably the same light in which he contemplated his live subject. Rodin told Dujardin-Beaumetz:

> The statue is transformed under the light, like everything that has volume; the atmosphere imposes successive transformations upon it. . . . Light separates, disjoins, decomposes, destroys false forms, be they rounded or thin; but when it shines on exact modelling, it gives the work the aspect and character of life.

The upraised arms initiate a radiant passage of light that flows to the knees. Seen in half the light, the face does not show the rougher, even brutalized realization that distinguished it from the firm finish of the body. Whether this discrepancy in mode relates to the model herself, to some thematic idea (the figure was destined for the lintel of *The Gates* among the damned), or to Rodin's fascination with conjoining the lyrical and grotesque is hard to say. Another example of the conjunction of incongruities, so often found in Rodin's art, is the disparity between the finish of the body and the roughly realized hands, which are suspended in air rather than touching each other or the hair. That this figure was to be seen frontally in the lintel of *The Gates* might explain the difference, and yet Rodin made no changes when it was separated from *The Gates*. He did put another, more cosmetically attractive head on the torso in a second version of *The Kneeling Faun*.

Rodin transformed *The Kneeling Faun* into *Orpheus with the Furies* by the device of tying a lyre to its chest. The Furies, who in the story destroy Orpheus, are here the pair of 'shades' seen above *The Kneeling Faun* in the lintel of *The Gates*. In this old photograph Rodin had placed some cloth across the legs of the kneeling figure to test the desirability of adding drapery to the composition. Neither the drapery nor the lyre appear in the bronze version in the Tokyo National Museum of Western Art.

100. *Orpheus Imploring the Gods.* 1892(?) Plaster.

In the bronze version, the floating figure of the woman does not appear. In plaster the woman is *The Martyr*, and Orpheus is the offspring of *The Prodigal Son* with changes in the legs and the left arm holding the instrument. The upper portion of *The Martyr* shows evidence of a base now *on* rather than *under* her back. Rodin may have put the base under *The Martyr* when he transposed the figure from a vertical to a horizontal position after its extraction from *The Gates of Hell*, or when he considered using it for the enlargement that Henri Lebossé was working on in 1900.

The Orpheus theme, so popular with Symbolist artists, was compelling for Rodin, not simply for being a tragic love story, but because of its relevance to the artist's profession. One of the most oft-repeated themes in his art is that of the artist and

his muse: the love or remoteness of inspiration, always personified by a woman. We do not know the exact date when Rodin assembled and manipulated his *Orpheus Imploring the Gods*, but if Grappe is correct and it is from 1892, the sculpture may reflect Rodin's agonies over his impending or actual separation from Camille Claudel, his mistress and artistic collaborator.

101–102. *Orpheus and Eurydice Leaving Hell.* Before 1889. Plaster. 1893. Marble. (Metropolitan Museum of Art).

Too often confined to museum reserves in recent years, except in the Paris Rodin Museum, since his death Rodin's marbles have been seen even by most of the artist's supporters as embarrassments to his achievement. Victims of a puritanical truth-to-the-medium aesthetic, observed more in the breach than the letter, Rodin's works in stone are often dismissed as not by his hand and unmodern in their theatricality and sentimentality. Many present-day artists and critics are uncomfortable before the depiction of physical beauty and of feeling, as they might be on seeing someone who had the bad grace to be ill in public. Words like imagination, beauty and feeling are banished from the vocabulary of formalists or used as epithets.

To look upon the finest of his marbles, such as this one (Plate 102, long in storage at the Metropolitan Museum of Art in New York), is to forget these partisan rejections. Rodin expressed it well to Paul Gsell: 'When after mature reflection you have laid down prohibitions which seem most reasonable in the matter of art, you will rightly reproach the mediocre man because he does not submit to them, but you will be surprised to observe that the man of genius infringes them almost with impunity.' Rodin was mindful of complaints after 1900 that his work was dependent upon literature and not thematically self-sufficient. To Paul Gsell he said: '. . . it is better . . . that the works of painters and sculptors should contain all their interest in themselves without recourse to literature. Instead of illustrating scenes from poems, it need only use plain symbols which do not require any written text. Such has generally been my method.'

More frequently than not, literary titles came after the artistic fact in Rodin's work. Although speaking of his *Centauress*, Rodin's views clarify his hopes for such as the *Orpheus* piece:

> In themes of this kind, the thought, I believe, is easily read. They awaken the imagination of the spectators without any outside help. And yet, far from confining it in narrow limits, they give it free rein to roam at will. That is . . . the role of art. The form which it creates ought only to furnish a pretext for the unlimited development of emotion.

Rodin's manner of working, with a few exceptions such as *The Kiss*, was to make a provocative coupling of figures and in the process or afterwards to find correspondences with literary themes. He told Gsell: 'You must not attribute too much

180

importance to the themes that you interpret. Without doubt they have value and help to charm the public; but the principal care of the artist should be to form living muscles. The rest matters little.' The plaster version of *Orpheus and Eurydice Leaving Hell* was assembled by 1889, when the artist Raffaelli did a portrait of the artist working on it. Eurydice comes from *The Martyr*, and the torso of Orpheus is found as a separate sculpture, while the legs recall those used for *Adam*. Orpheus's right arm looks almost identical with that of Eurydice, while his left arm and head have only been roughed out in plaster rather than modelled first in clay. Perhaps Rodin anticipated the translation into marble and left it to his *practicien* to 'form living muscles' in the legs and arm under his guidance. The stone background behind this pair was not casually arrived at but carefully thought out as to shape, proportion and size, as well as texture. The shadows they throw on the rock evoke the exit from Hades. In the photograph there is a provocative and felicitous conjunction of the shape of the marble against that of *The Age of Bronze* at the left.

103. *Christ and Mary Magdalene*. Original version in plaster 1894. Marble version 1903.

Although it appears to have been destroyed during his lifetime, a large crucified Christ is reported to have been made by Rodin in the 1880s. There is no way of knowing how the figure of Christ in this marble sculpture, sold to Baron von Thyssen, relates to its predecessor. The Magdalene is a reworking of the figure of Meditation made for *The Gates of Hell*. Grappe and others report that this composition began as an image of a bound Prometheus and an Oceanid consoling him. More than once Rodin identified with the mythical hero of the artist's profession, and it is probable that this composition was a self-portrait at a critical moment in his career and private life. The work was first modelled in clay, and the stunning 1894 plaster cast has been in the Meudon Reserve for many years, if not since the artist's death. Neither of two marbles carved from it match the plaster in intensity of feeling or brutality and brilliance of modelling.

   In the early 1890s, Rodin was going through professional and personal experiences that were traumatic. There had been severe criticism and rejection of his models for monuments to Victor Hugo and Balzac. His *Monument to Claude Lorrain* had been bitterly faulted, causing the artist, in a rare concession to his critics, to rework the marble socle. *The Burghers of Calais* was still awaiting installation. His personal life was in chaos with the tragic break he had made with Camille Claudel, who had been his mistress, model and assistant for ten years. It is not hard to imagine Rodin identifying with the suffering Christ-Prometheus figure and imagining himself as crucified or bound by work and love. Camille Claudel was supposed to have modelled for the figure of Meditation, which became the grieving Magdalene. This was just the situation to inspire one of his least-known but greatest works. Some years later he told Paul Gsell that the artist finds inspiration even in suffering:

Christ and Mary Magdalene. Plaster, 1894. Meudon Reserve. Photo Bruno Jarret, 1979

At times his own heart is on the rack, yet stronger than pain is the bitter joy which he experiences in understanding and giving expression to that pain. Upon his own anguish, upon his own gaping wounds, he fixes the enthusiastic gaze of the man who has read the decrees of fate.

In the marble versions, Christ is crucified on a wooden cross that seems set into or is part of a rock, thereby also recalling Prometheus chained to the rock and Christ's entombment in a cave. His posture is such that the upper half of his body enacts the Crucifixion, while the legs, touching the earth, evoke the Deposition. The Magdalene, whose nudity is her symbol and passion, embraces the figure and also seems to assist in lowering the body. (In the original plaster she does not actually touch the body.) There is no direct sculptural precedent for such an erotic conception, but Rodin may have known Felicien Rops's frontispiece for Rodolphe Darzen's *L'Amante du Christ* (the drawing of which is in the Stanford University Art Museum), wherein a naked Magdalene crouches at the feet of Christ, whose blood falls on to her body. The more brutal realism of the plaster Christ may have been encouraged not only by Rodin's admiration for late medieval French art, but also by his having seen the chapel of Santisimo Cristo at Burgos, whose dying saviour he likened to a corpse.

104–106. *The Hand of God.* 1898(?)

107. Rodin with *The Hand of God.* 1902(?)

According to Georges Grappe, the first realization of this famous sculpture was achieved by 1898, when the writer Eduard Rod visited the artist and recorded what he saw. Athena Spear correctly points out that the great hand is from one of *The Burghers of Calais*, the one known in Rodin's lifetime as 'Le Passant' and in recent years as Pierre de Wiessant (see Plate 55). Set into the hand are Adam and Eve, the sleeping woman being embraced by the male, whose form is overlapped by hers. They appear to have been created just for this composition. Both are shown as if partly attached to a rock, suggesting the divine gift of life from inert matter. Perhaps this idea was Rodin's answer to the criticism of his excessive use of unfinished stone. Rodin referred to God as a modeller; Michelangelo likened Him to a carver. Unlike its medieval prototype, in which God's hand descends from the heavens, Rodin's hand of God was visualized by the artist, as we can see from contemporary photographs, not only thrusting upward as if from the earth, but outward, as if from a mountain, or rising in a diagonal thrust, as it does in a bronze version in the Cleveland Museum of Art. Each shift of axis alters the meaning, so that the horizontal gesture, for example, is like an offering. The photograph of Rodin in a smock next to *The Hand of God* is one of the best in capturing the sense of the toll sculpture took on the artist; it could be captioned, 'He was a worker.' Rodin made several replicas of the work in stone and bronze. Shortly before his death he caused a life-cast to be made of his own hand, into which he set the torso of a woman, thereby recalling his vindication from charges of *surmoulage*, offering the future the legacy of the partial figure, and equating the sculptor with God.

108–109. *The Kiss.* 1886. Marble version 1898.

The Kiss is Rodin's most literary piece, directly inspired by Dante's *Inferno*. In the circle of carnal sinners Vergil leads the poet to Paolo and Francesca, and the latter speaks to them:

> One day for pastime, we read of Lancelot, how love constrained him; we were alone, without all suspicion. Several times that reading urged our eyes to meet, and changed the colour of our faces; but one moment alone it was that overcame us. When we read how the fond smile was kissed by such a lover, he, who shall never be divided from me, kissed my mouth all trembling.

The lovers were then surprised by Francesca's husband, who slew them both. From the first moments devoted to planning the motifs in *The Gates of Hell*, Rodin seems to have determined to depict this tragic couple. His many drawings of the pair and their inclusion in the last maquette for the door testify to his commitment. It is also probable that the first small version of *The Kiss* was modelled as early as 1880 or 1881. The decision to exclude the couple from *The Gates* may have been due to Rodin's desire to eliminate, in Rilke's words, 'everything that was too solitary to subject itself to the great totality'. In 1887, Rodin exhibited the half-life-size plaster both in Paris and Brussels, but without a title. It was called *The Lovers* by some writers, but the one who named it *The Kiss*, because, according to Grappe, he thought Houdon would have supplied that title, had the satisfaction of successfully baptizing the work. It was shown in Germany in 1897 under the title *Intimacy* and later *Adam and Eve*. Rodin was commissioned by the French government to have the plaster carved in marble, and it was first shown to the public in the May Salon of 1898 in the place of honour, some fifty feet from the *Balzac*. (Rodin's *praticien*, Jean Turcan, did the enlargement and carving.) Rodin told his friend, the writer Charles Morice, about the moment when the marble was removed from the studio on the way to the Salon:

> When my marble group of *The Kiss* was carried out, it passed in front of *Balzac* that I had left expressly in the courtyard in order to see it against an empty sky. I was not unhappy with the simplified vigour of my marble. Nevertheless, when it passed, I had the sensation that it was soft, that it fell before the other. . . .

Rodin was quoted in the 1 November 1907 issue of *La Revue* as saying:

> Without doubt the interlacing of *The Kiss* is pretty, but in this group I did not find anything. It is a theme treated according to the tradition of the School; a subject complete in itself and artificially isolated from the world which surrounds it.

When first exhibited and then later shown in the 1898 exhibition, *The Kiss* received great public approval, although its nudity shocked some who were unaware of the story and thought the figures depicted their own contemporaries. *The Kiss* did much to earn Rodin the reputation of a sculptor of the erotic. He handled the embrace with the utmost tact; the lips are not yet touching, and Paolo's right hand rests tentatively on Francesca's thigh, while the left still holds the book behind her back. One can sense conflicting feelings in Paolo's body; he was the brother of his lover's husband, who had asked him to tutor Francesca. It is Francesca who seems the most ardent, and it is she who slings her leg across that of her partner (in what Leo Steinberg has dubbed 'the slung-leg motif') as a symbol of desired sexual intimacy. Past, present and future are suggested by Rodin, who believed that sculpture should show successive states of being as well as movement. *The Kiss* contradicts the view that lacking a Beaux-Arts education Rodin never learned to compose, and its 'pretty' interlacing helps us understand the position he departed from in the figural couplings.

The great photographs by Druet, taken in the studio perhaps when he first worked for Rodin, tend to overcome that fault Rodin commented on when he saw the marble couple out of doors: that artificial isolation from the world around them. A mallet stands on the floor in this photograph, although in later prints it was unfortunately removed. On the saddle at the right is a small dish which probably held the matrix for the marble dust used to fill the holes in the marble left when unmetamorphosed grains of sand fell out. Placing the figures by a window in the shadows with the mallet evokes the Pygmalion theme popular in the 1890s and treated elsewhere by Rodin. We see the figures as he would have us see them, and it is possible to enjoy the big planes and simplified vigour of which he approved.

110–117. The *Monument to Balzac*. 1896–7.

One of the great dramas of modern sculpture was the evolution of Rodin's *Monument to Balzac* from a portrait of a writer to a symbol of creation. Perhaps no single work before or after has received as vehement a rejection upon its public appearance; and one is hard put to imagine a comparable investment of thought and feeling as well as labour in a single statue. From the outset, in 1891, when he received the commission from the Société des Gens de Lettres, Rodin sought what he called 'an honest work'. This meant one for which he

Study for the robe of *Balzac*. Plaster, 1897. Photo Druet, gelatin silver print, 25.1 × 18 cm (cat. no. 1379)

would steep himself in the writer's appearance at various ages and in the writings that were the key to his thought and spirit. The Musée Rodin archives do not yield photographs of figural studies earlier than that reproduced in Plate 111, which probably dates from 1896, Rodin's second great campaign to satisfy his commissioners. Druet photographed what seems superficially an academic pose struck by a heavily muscled model. (Rodin worked out the head separately from the torso, which explains the partial figure in this photograph by Druet.) One of the model's hands, in fact, grasps his penis, an auto-erotic gesture that Rodin may have felt was appropriate to a creator. The folded arms under the robe were intended to have given the impression of Balzac's considerable girth. This half-sized figural study became the body beneath the *robe de chambre* in the final sculpture. Plate 112 shows one of several studies in plaster for that robe with the armatures clearly visible. In the summer of 1897, Rodin had Lebossé enlarge his *Balzac*, and photographs show us the upper half. Pencil marks are discernible in the area of the neck, about which Rodin said to Chincholle in May 1898:

> The only thing that I realize today is that the neck is too strong. I thought I had to enlarge it because according to me, modern sculpture must exaggerate the forms from the moral point of view. Through this exaggerated neck I wanted to represent strength. I realize that the execution exceeded the idea.

Despite his lament that he wanted more time to study his *Balzac*, Rodin had the final work in his studio from at least July 1897 until it left for the Salon at the end of April 1898. He was so concerned that he asked Lebossé to get the opinion of his estranged mistress and former assistant, Camille Claudel. On the eve of the exhibition she wrote a note now in the Musée Rodin archives:

> Through Lebossé you have asked that I write you my opinion of your statue of Balzac. I find it very great and very beautiful, and best of all the studies of the same subject. Above all, the very accentuated effect of the head which contrasts with the simplicity of the drapery. It is a real discovery and gripping. I also like very much the waving sleeves, which have captured well the negligent aspect of the man. In sum, I believe you can expect a great success, above all from the true connoisseurs, who will not be able to make any comparison between this statue and those that up to now decorate the city of Paris.

We have some excellent photographs that show us how the *Balzac* looked in the Salon to a professional photographer guided by Rodin (Plate 110) and to an amateur (see opposite), who captured the crowd around it (the large foreground figure of a Sower was by Cordonier). Rodin kept the statue on view two weeks before removing it to Meudon because of its rejection by the commissioners. At Meudon, he invited several photographers to take pictures that captured his intentions. Bulloz did a series of beautiful views that show the viewpoints from which Rodin believed his work had suc-

Photograph of the crowd viewing the *Monument to Balzac* at the 1898 Salon. Photographer unknown, 4 × 5 cm (cat. no. 1332)

ceeded, including the back. He preferred Steichen's because they captured the sense of the sculpture belonging to the light and space around it. Photographs that show the obelisk-like silhouette also permit associations with phallic forms that, intentionally or not, seem appropriate to the theme.

Both photography and the artist's own words help us to know what he had in mind for this great sculpture. To Paul Gsell, he recalled the outraged criticisms:

By what right do they reproach this dressing-gown with its hanging, empty sleeves? Does an inspired writer dress otherwise when at night he walks feverishly in his apartment in pursuit of his private vision? This just wasn't done before. By convention, a statue in a public place must represent a great man in a theatrical attitude which will cause him to be admired by posterity. But such reasoning is absurd. I submit that there was only one way to evoke my subject. I had to show a Balzac in his study, breathless, hair in disorder, eyes lost in a dream, a genius who in his little room reconstructs piece by piece all of society in order to bring it into tumultuous life before his contemporaries and generations to come; Balzac truly heroic, who does not stop to rest for a moment, who makes night into day, who drives himself in vain to fill the gaps made by his debts, who above all dedicates himself to building an immortal monument, who is transported by passion, whose body is made frenetic and violent, and who does not heed the warnings of his diseased heart, from which he will soon die. It seems to me that such a Balzac, even seen in a public place, would be greater and more worthy of admiration than just any writer who sits in a chair or who proudly poses for the enthusiastic crowd. In sum, there is nothing more beautiful than the absolute truth of real existence.

118. Rodin working at Night. Date unknown.

This photograph complements the night study of Plate 117 and may have been taken at the same time. Rodin found not working to be 'odious', and Steichen recorded him making use of the night to study a sculpture by candlelight, calculating the rightness of the planes and their relationships, and seeing if the surfaces still came to life.

119. *The Mask of Hanako.* 1908. Clay.

In 1908, Rodin met the Japanese dancer, Ohta Hisa, also known as Hanako. He appreciated her astounding coordination, her ability to hold a difficult pose, and her joints, which were as thick as her limbs; and she posed for several drawings and figure studies. Judith Cladel, who observed these sessions, wrote in her 1918 book on Rodin:

I watched Rodin model the head of Hanako.... He rapidly modelled the whole in the rough, as he does all his busts. His keen eye and experienced thumb enable him to establish the exact dimensions at the first sitting. Then the work of detailed modelling begins. The sculptor is not satisfied to mould the mass in its apparent outlines only. With absolute accuracy he slices off some clay, cuts off the head of the bust, and lays it upside down on a cushion. He then makes his model lie on the couch. Bent like a vivisector over his subject, he studies the structure of the skull seen from above, the jaws viewed from below, and the lines which join the head to the throat, and the nape of the neck to the spine. Then he chisels the features with the point of a pen-knife, bringing out the recesses of the eyelids, the nostrils, the curves of the mouth.

Steichen, who was at Meudon in 1908, photographed two masks of Hanako in clay while they were presumably still wet. The lifelike quality of the whole is due both to the extraordinary modelling and to Steichen's close-up shot, in which the hair is slightly out of focus, as it would be if we were looking directly at the mask ourselves. In the Meudon Reserve there are three terracotta and plaster masks that undoubtedly derived from the works Steichen photographed. They are equal in size and approximately the same in overall shape, suggesting that they derived from a basic, probably calm expression. Cladel wrote:

In making a bust Rodin takes numerous clay impressions, according to the rate of progress. In this way he can revert to the impression of the previous day, if the last pose was not good, or if, in the language of the trade, 'he has overworked his material'. Thus one may see five, six or even eight similar heads in his studio, each with a different expression.

Cladel may have also described just the expression we see in Plate 119, for she says:

Hanako did not pose like other people. Her features were contracted in the expression of cold terrible rage. She had the look of a tiger, an expression thoroughly foreign to our Occidental countenances. With the force of will which the Japanese display in the face of death, Hanako was enabled to hold this look for hours.

120. *Georges Clemenceau.* 1911. Bronze(?)

In 1911, the Argentine government commissioned Rodin to model a portrait of Clemenceau, intended as a gift to the great French statesman. At the time their friendship of some years had cooled because of Rodin's refusal to side with the Dreyfusards, a cause strongly championed by Clemenceau. The latter's great respect for the artist caused him to sit patiently through innumerable sittings. (One writer has said that twenty-three studies were made in eighteen sittings, but we found thirteen in the Meudon Reserve.) What drove Rodin to make so many studies was not the problem of resemblance, but, as with the *Balzac*, his desire to go beyond a likeness to an evocation of a spirit that was like a clenched fist. Clemenceau rejected the studies and the final version, particularly since he felt the last made him look like a Mongolian general.

The bond between Rodin and his photographers was their joy in and love of light as the means by which they could achieve expression. Steichen limns Rodin's *Clemenceau* by moonlight in a photograph, one of a series that to my knowledge has not been reproduced before. In some ways this photograph is more daring than those of *Balzac*, as so much of the head, which almost fills the field, is in shadow. Close inspection of the print, however, shows that the shadows have not totally obliterated the major modelling planes. One has the impression that just as Rodin saw his art as a continuum; Steichen was taking up where Rodin had left off.

121. *The Head of Sorrow* or *Joan of Arc.* 1907. (Ny Carlsberg Glyptothek)

If one head from *The Gates of Hell* expresses the spirit of the whole – and that spirit is a cry of world anguish – it is *The Head of Sorrow*. This head has served the figure of *The Prodigal Son*, Paolo in *Paolo and Francesca*, and one of the sons of Ugolino, all in the portal. The bisexual nature of the head allowed Rodin to title it severally *Medusa*, *Joan of Arc* and *Orpheus*. The faggots which appear in the marble in this photograph suggest *Joan of Arc* is depicted here.

On his trip to Rome in 1875, Rodin visited the Vatican Museum and probably the Terme Museum as well, and he could have seen the Laöcoön and Niobid groups, whose expressions of despair may have fostered *The Head of Sorrow*. Its first appearance in connection with a dying son of Ugolino evokes recollections of a dying child of Niobe. Rodin's head has no stylistic parentage in antiquity, for when he went to life, he felt he had penetrated the sources of all style, especially that of the Greeks. Bulloz's splendid photograph makes it seem as if Rodin has modelled his head out of light.

122. *Eve Fairfax* or *The Amazon.* 1905(?)

Rodin admired the beauty and poise of his English women clients, and of Miss Eve Fairfax, who posed for him in 1902 and 1903, he said, 'A Diana and a Satyr in one'. He told Jacques-Émile Blanche, 'How flat-chested they are – oh, those planes and the body structure of these English women!' At the age of ninety-eight Eve Fairfax recalled:

He was a remarkable man – very charming, kind and a dedicated artist. We spent the modelling sessions speaking to each other, I in broken French. . . . Rodin liked me very much. . . . He found me refreshing because at the time he was very popular and many French women were running after him. I think I appealed to him because . . . I was not prepared to jump into bed with him at every occasion. . . .

The portrait had been commissioned by Miss Fairfax's fiancé and was cancelled when the engagement was broken off. Rodin chose to continue, titling the work *The Amazon*, and caused several versions to be carved in stone.

Bulloz's superb photograph as much as the sculpture captures that quality of the 'soul portrait' that so appealed to his society patrons, and we can understand how reproduction of this photograph increased demand for Rodin's portraits. The marble seems to come alive through the side-lighting, which recalls Rodin's comments to Dujardin-Beaumetz:

The statue is transformed under the light, like everything that has volume; the atmosphere imposes successive transformations upon it. Thus it is important for the work to approach closely to reality, and then the colorations arrange and distribute themselves, play upon true forms, consequently upon exact contours. Light separates, disjoins, decomposes, destroys false forms . . . but when it shines on exact modelling it gives the work the aspect and character of life.

Both this statement and the portrait of Eve Fairfax itself indicate that Rodin was not an Impressionist, because he did not depict the disintegrating action of light on form, but rather through exact contours sought to resist decomposition.

123–124. *Barbey d'Aurevilly.* 1909. Plaster.

It was twenty years after the death of the diabolist writer and dandy, Jules-Amédée Barbey d'Aurevilly, who had rebelled against and then rejoined the Church, that Rodin did this spirited portrait intended for a monument in Saint-Sauveur-le-Vicomte, Normandy. The sculptor worked from photographs that showed the novelist in a costume of his own design admired by *fin-de-siècle* Symbolists, such as Sar Péladan. Rodin rejected the hood, but kept the sense of the outer gown, so that the prow-like head projects upward, as if from a sea of agitated shapes. This dualistic mode of modelling, which contrasts with his portraits of the eighties, can be seen in many of Rodin's late portraits in all media. Perhaps he favoured the light-trapping irregular borders and surfaces which would counter the appearance of self-enclosure. Unlike the portraits done by Medardo Rosso, with which that of Barbey had some affinities, this work was intended by Rodin to be scrutinized from all sides, as we can see from the clay additions to the plaster, which deny the deceptive casualness of the facture.

When asked by chemistry students to make a bust of the late Pierre Curie, Rodin wrote of the problems of doing a posthumous portrait:

> In principle, to make a bust with no other documents than photographs is always a difficult thing for me. Living nature alone can create a strong and beautiful bust, for the sculptor does not invent, he only takes the forces of nature, and only his faithfulness in reproducing it allows him to give a strength of expression which he himself does not always absolutely understand. The living play of the features explains to him, by stirring it, the passivity of calm and repose.

125. The proposed *Monument to Puvis de Chavannes*. 1899– c. 1907. Plaster.

In his 1907 lecture on Rodin, Rilke described the sculptor's studio and noted what is shown in this photograph:

> I was passing through the vast workshops, lost in thought, and I noticed everything was in a state of growth and that nothing was in a hurry. There stood the Thinker in bronze, mightily concentrated within himself, completed; but he was part of the still growing complexity of the Gate of Hell. There was one of the monuments of Victor Hugo, advancing slowly towards completion, still under observation, still liable perhaps to alteration, and further off stood the other versions still incomplete. There lay the Ugolino group, like the unearthed roots of an ancient oak, waiting. There was waiting the remarkable monument for Puvis de Chavannes with the table, the apple tree, and the glorious spirit of eternal peace. And over yonder was what I took to be a monument for Whistler.

There was no living artist more admired by Rodin than Puvis de Chavannes. Reportedly the sculptor's last words were to praise Puvis over his critics. Before the monument had been proposed, Rodin had already created a bust of Puvis. Only a respect verging on awe caused him to clothe the bust *à l'antique*, as the painter requested, on the eve of its first public exhibition in 1891. In 1899, a committee of the National Society of Fine Arts, headed by Carolus-Duran, its president, commissioned Rodin to create a monument to Puvis to be located in the new square of Cluny. The commission must have been received with mixed feelings by Rodin, already overcommitted to monumental projects and still inwardly suffering from what he termed the 'defeat' of his *Balzac*. In 1902, he showed the committee his earlier bust of Puvis, intended for marble, and a muse, *The Spirit of Eternal Repose*, that Grappe dates to 1898. The bust was to surmount an architectural stele, and Rodin estimated the project would be

finished by 1904. In 1910, newspapers carried the information that the monument would be completed that year and that the bust had been carved in marble. In 1913, Rodin exhibited the bust in '*pierre brute*' along with the *Muse* in plaster. According to Grappe, this figure reached only as far as the '*saumon*' or roughed-out stage in stone. Rilke's description matches that of this photograph, and the table and apple tree seem not to have figured in the proposed monument after 1910. (The apple tree covered with plaster sits in the Meudon Reserve.) As with other unfinished monuments, Rodin seems not to have discussed the reasons for not completing them. Contemporary commentators noted that he preferred to exhibit his partial figures, and undoubtedly he put his heart into his *études* after 1900. Not surprisingly, recent commentators have repeated the view that he was incapable of thinking in monumental terms, as if *The Burghers of Calais* and *Balzac* were not artistically successful monuments. Rodin had determined not to think in terms of conventional monuments, which he could have realized. He was accused in his lifetime and has been since of being too uncritical of his work, permitting '*pâtisseries*' to escape from his studio in profusion. Perhaps his problem was that he was too critical of his monumental projects and too dedicated to trying to be original in revitalizing the public monument. The argument that he may have begun to feel that in this new century monuments were inappropriate is not persuasive, as witness his devotion to Puvis.

126. The Muse for the *Monument to Whistler*. 1905–10. Plaster.

It was two years after Whistler's death in 1903, that Rodin, who had succeeded to the presidency of the International Society of Sculptors, Painters and Gravers, agreed to do a monument to his friend. It was proposed to Rodin that the subject be a 'Winged Victory symbolizing Whistler's triumph – the triumph of Art over its enemies'. During the next few years he made a few drawings and some small models, all of the Muse, which Lebossé enlarged in the plaster shown in this photograph. In the 1908 Salon Rodin exhibited his armless Muse, seen as if climbing the mountain of fame or bracing her leg while pondering Whistler's medallion portrait. Rodin had earlier considered having the Muse drawing or holding a portrait of Whistler. It seems from the archives that Lebossé completed one of the arms for the Muse in 1909, after having enlarged the legs, torso and head. A flood in 1910 damaged the lower portion of the big plaster, and he was obliged to redo the drapery. In the photograph one can see that he immersed heavy cloth in wet plaster to effect the drapery. The model for the head and possibly for the body of the muse was the young English artist, Gwen Mary John, sister of Augustus John. She came to study and work with Rodin in 1905, and later became his mistress. (Her erotic letters to the artist in the Rodin Museum are signed 'Mary John'.) Rodin's own self-imposed demands for originality in monuments and the fact that he was, as he put it, 'a hard man to satisfy' combined with the crushing claims on his time from all sources, his advancing age, and perhaps his greater interest in partial figures, to doom this and other monuments to incompletion. (For a thorough history of the project see the article in the December 1978 *Gazette des Beaux-Arts*, 'Rodin: The Whistler Monument,' by Joy Newton and Margaret MacDonald.)

127. *Ariadne* or *Reclining Woman*. Before 1899, enlargement 1905. Plaster.
128. *Cybele* or *Seated Woman*. 1899, enlargement 1905. Plaster.
129. *Torso of a Young Woman*. 1909. Plaster.
130. *Prayer.* 1909. Plaster.
131. *Punishment* or *Châtiment*. 1912. Plaster.

Rodin learned as a student to make sculpture by modelling parts of the human figure. He drew from ancient fragments and owned, at first, plaster casts of broken ancient statuary. When he became affluent, he purchased large quantities of ancient torsos, hands and feet. From the 1870s, if not earlier, it was his practice to re-use favoured torsos, such as that of *Adèle*. In the Meudon Reserve there are some small armless figures that from their style seem to have been done before 1880. Rodin's practice of completing a sculpture by unmaking it derived from accidents and from calculated decisions, as in *The Man with the Broken Nose* and *The Age of Bronze*. In the first sculpture it was accident that shaped the work, and in the second he removed the spear that would have finished it. He would edit figures severely, cutting away without replacement portions of the body he felt were unsuccessfully modelled or enlarged. He even masked with cloth those portions of ancient torsos he owned that he felt were of inferior modelling. Occasionally, his partial figures had a thematic intent, as in the case of *La Terre*, which evoked life coming into being from raw matter. Rodin's work on *The Gates of Hell* gave the strongest impetus to his reflections on the artistic completeness of a well-made figural part or partial figure. Meditations on ancient fragments convinced him that beauty and perfection could be found in the part, whereas to the ancient Greeks this conception would have been unthinkable. On the basis of his own work and his observation of ancient predecessors, he could say to Gsell, 'When a good sculptor models a torso, he not only represents the muscles, but the life which animates them – more than the life, the force that fashioned them, it may be, grace or strength, or amorous charm, or indomitable will.'

By 1889, Rodin was exhibiting partial figures, which he called *études*, and there were a large number in his 1900 exhibition. In the 1890s he had some of his partial figures, such as *Iris, Messenger of the Gods*, enlarged by Lebossé, a decisive indication that he thought they were complete. By exhibiting in the late 1890s some of these figures, among them *Seated Woman* and *Meditation*, Rodin was further challenging the conventions of sculptural finish by proposing a concept of completeness that would have been recognized by Baudelaire, who had written in 1845 in his essay 'Art in Paris':

A work of genius . . . in which every element is well seen, well observed, well understood and well imagined, will always be well executed when it is sufficiently so. Next, that there is a great difference between a work that is complete and a work that is finished; that in general what is complete is not finished, and that a thing that is highly finished need not be complete at all.

In a letter to William Rothenstein, 17 November 1900, Rodin wrote of the fragmented Burgher exhibited in the portico of the pavilion, 'It is complete [Rodin's underlining] even if the exhibited *morceau* is without head and hands. This figure has a great *désinvolture*.'

A second poet, Rilke, who had occasion to observe Rodin's partial figures closely, wrote in 1903:

The same completeness is conveyed in all the armless statues of Rodin; nothing necessary is lacking. One stands before them as before something whole. The feeling of incompleteness does not arise from the mere aspect of a thing, but from the assumption of a narrow-minded pedantry which says that arms are as necessary a part of the body and that a body without arms cannot be perfect. . . . With regard to the painter, at least, came the understanding and the belief that an artistic whole need not necessarily coincide with the complete thing . . . that new values, proportions and balances may originate within the pictures. In the art of sculpture, also, it is left to the artist to make out of many things one thing, and from the smallest part of a thing an entirety.

In defence of his partial figures Rodin cited the long history of portraiture, and after 1900 he exhibited only portraits and figures enlarged by Lebossé, which were, with the exception of *The Thinker*, partial figures. An eye-witness to the reactions that followed was Judith Cladel, whose statement in her book of 1908 strongly suggests exposure to Rodin's own comments:

The master has exhibited his *morceaux* and they have evoked from his critics the rudest criticism. These critics have never wanted to comprehend that he has not delivered to them works that were properly decorative but rather the unique beauty of métier which appears here more thrilling than in his most finished sculptures. . . . Nothing veils or covers them, neither the interest of the subject, nor the expression of sentiment or feeling. All that is there is the quality of modelling, the raw result of work. In reality it is not Iris, The Earth, The Muse, but torsos which appear to be fragments of a destroyed movement; it is the sum of art, a certificate that the sculptor gives himself, the total of his efforts and researches concentrated in plastic formulas. Therefore, of what importance is it to him to achieve details or a seductive arrangement? Who contemplates these works must do it with the *esprit du savant* before a *morceau* of nature to be studied and not with the attitude of a dilettante looking for aesthetic pleasure and the emotion of the subject that does not exist.

As Zola admonished that one must forget a thousand things about painting before a painting by Manet, so Rodin asks through Cladel that the public forget a thousand things about sculpture. He would have qualified her last statement, however, as his great torsos, such as that of *The Young Woman*, burst with exuberant life.

Rodin's exhibition of his *études* in the 1880s and their inspection by visitors to his studios did not always evoke adverse criticism, for English critics by 1883 were championing Rodin as the world's greatest master of the sculptural *morceau*. There is no doubt, however, that he was mindful of strong animosity towards his views when he talked with Bartlett in the late 1880s:

> I am an inventor. . . . I deliver the results of my researches in *morceaux*, which are the studies of planes and modelling. I am reproached for not personally showing all the applications which result from them. Let those who follow me occupy themselves with this task. I must content myself with having led the intelligence of the artist of my time into the environment of Michelangelo and the Antique. When Volta discovered the electric pile, he could not himself give all of its applications, which since have upset all of science. . . . A well-made torso contains all of life. One doesn't add anything by joining arms and legs to it. My *morceaux* are the examples that I propose for the study of other artists. They are not finished, it is said. And the cathedrals, are they finished?

In 1912, after the exhibition of the partial figures here reproduced, Rodin further explained his intentions in addressing the artist Michel Georges-Michel:

> Have not the public and critics who serve the public reproached me enough for exhibiting simple parts of the body? . . . These people comprehend nothing of sculpture, or what is an *étude*. They cannot imagine that an artist must apply himself to giving as much expression to a hand or a torso as to a face and that it is logical for an artist to exhibit an arm rather than a bust arbitrarily deprived by tradition of arms, legs and abdomen. Expression and proportion, the ends are there. The means are modelling. It is by modelling that flesh lives, vibrates, struggles and suffers.

Listed in the Salon of 1905 as *A Figure*, the reclining woman illustrated in Plate 127 was elsewhere referred to by Rodin as *Ariadne*, and she served as the maquette for a tomb sculpture that he never finished in marble. The plaster in the Salon lacks arms, perhaps because he exhibited the work while Lebossé was enlarging it or perhaps because he found the contracted form more compelling. *Cybele* or *The Seated Woman* (Plate 128) was first exhibited in its original smaller size in 1897, and its enlargement was shown in 1905 and 1914. The model for both figures was Madame Abruzzezzi, one of Rodin's favourite models. In 1894, when she was arrested for

poisoning her husband, Rodin defended her, and he helped her financially when she retired from modelling. Rodin's assistants named the reclining figure 'Abruzzezzi Reclining', and the other, 'Abruzzezzi Seated'.

Torso of a Young Woman (Plate 129) is an enlargement of a smaller sculpture; the mound-like shape on the thighs suggest that at one time she had arms and hands, which touched her legs. Grappe believed that the original small version of *Prayer* (Plate 130) derived from *The Gates* but was not included in it. The Meudon Reserve contains an old small plaster cast of this figure, which is one of the closest to the ancient Greek torsos that Rodin made.

Punishment or *Châtiment* (Plate 131), probably named after a poem by Victor Hugo, is the penultimate figure sculpture Rodin publicly exhibited. In 1914, he re-exhibited *Cybele*. I have found no trace of *Punishment* in the Meudon Reserve nor the Musée Rodin as a whole, and, to my knowledge, it does not appear in the Rodin literature. Lebossé, writing to Rodin on 30 January 1912, indicated that he was working on the enlargement '*de votre joli groupe Châtiment*' from a small model. He indicated that his atelier was too small for Rodin to judge the effects of the *ensemble* and recommended transporting it to one of Rodin's studios, where it could be properly studied and modified. Further, Lebossé urged that to facilitate transport, the attached *figures* be sectioned, since they were without arms or connecting irons, and then carefully reassembled. Thus, the figure exhibited in 1912 indicates that Rodin had decided not to show the group. Was the title inspired by the proximity of a man and woman, both of whom lacked arms?

132–134. *The Walking Man.* Enlargement 1905. Plaster.

The complex history of *The Walking Man* reflects Rodin's practice of making small-scale studies of parts of a proposed statue, assembling them in various ways at different times, revising earlier rather than later versions of a figural part, and then enlarging his new synthesis. In 1878 he made a study of a torso destined for the *John the Baptist Preaching*. This severely edited torso was then reworked into a half life-size, armless, but full length study of the prophet, which was recently identified in the Meudon Reserve. Rodin caused the original torso to be bronze cast and it was exhibited in 1889. In 1900, he presumably joined a new clay cast of the original torso that had been kept in plaster and is at Meudon, to clay casts of the legs from the half-size study of *The Baptist* after elongating the trailing left leg in order to evoke a greater impression of forward movement. He then exhibited in plaster this half life-size sculpture as *The Walking Man* at his 1900 retrospective. In 1905, Lebossé enlarged the work to more than life-size, and in 1907 the plaster was the 'clou' or featured sculpture in a Salon. This public exhibition and photographic reproduction of *The Walking Man* exerted a profound and far-reaching influence on many younger modern sculptors. In 1912, at the invitation of the French government, Rodin sent the first bronze cast to Rome, where it was installed in a socle in the courtyard of the Farnese Palace that housed the French embassy. The ambassador disliked the sculpture and had it returned on the grounds that it obstructed traffic. By cropping the sculpture's base and photographing it off-centre, Haweis and Coles interpreted *The Walking Man* as if striding through the world at night.

135. *A Couple*. Date unknown. Plaster.
136. *A Couple in a Small Urn*. Date unknown. Plaster.

In two of the most poetic photographs ever taken of Rodin's sculpture, an unknown photographer, presumably under Rodin's direction, staged two paired figures, bringing them together in the one case by propping them against each other, and in the other by placing them in an ancient urn or cup. After 1900, Rodin enjoyed using small objects from his growing collection of antiquities as bases for his sculptures. A large number of these montages are in the Meudon Reserve, testimony to the artist's playful spirit in bridging past and present.

137. Rodin Conversing With Henri Lebossé at Meudon. 1912(?)

The sculptor is shown with one of his most important assistants in the studio attached to his home at Meudon. (The endpapers of this book show the other end of his studio.) The photograph may have been taken about 1912. Henri Lebossé did most of Rodin's enlargements and reductions from about 1894 until the artist's death. (Lebossé's correspondence with Rodin in the Musée Rodin archives begins in 1894.) Lebossé was a remarkable technician, loyal, proud, and always responsive to Rodin's exacting demands. He carried out his work on equipment derived from the Collas machine invented in 1836, equipment still in use by a Paris artisan today. The last life-size works completed entirely by Rodin appear to have been *The Burghers of Calais*. After at least 1894, Lebossé was responsible for the famous enlargements of such works as *The Thinker* and *The Walking Man* and all of the other partial figures exhibited after 1900. He prided himself on being able to reproduce all but Rodin's fingerprints.

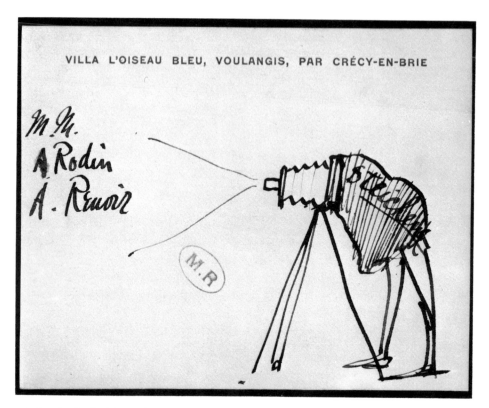

A drawing by Steichen of himself taking a photograph, presumably of Rodin and Renoir, whose names are on the left. The drawing is on a postcard from Steichen to Rodin (cat. no. 2162)

Bibliography

Biographical books

CLADEL, JUDITH, *Rodin, sa vie glorieuse, sa vie inconnue*, Édition définitive, Grasset, 1950. (This remains the best biography.)

DESCHARNES, ROBERT, and CHABRUN, JEAN-FRANÇOIS, *Auguste Rodin*, Macmillan, 1967. (Good biographical and excellent photographic coverage of Rodin's work.)

LAWTON, FREDERICK, *The Life and Work of August Rodin*, Unwin, 1906. (An informative collection by one of Rodin's secretaries.)

LUDOVICI, ANTHONY, *Personal Reminiscences of Auguste Rodin*, Lippincott, 1926. (An interesting biography by one of Rodin's secretaries.)

SUTTON, DENYS, *Triumphant Satyr: The World of Auguste Rodin*, Penguin, 1963. (A good biography with a bad title.)

Catalogues

BOWNESS, ALAN, *Rodin*, Arts Council of Great Britain, 1969.

DE CASO, JACQUES, and SANDERS, PATRICIA, *Rodin's Sculpture: A Critical Study of the Spreckels Collection, California Palace of the Legion of Honor*, 1977. (An excellent catalogue.)

ELSEN, ALBERT E., *The Partial Figure in Modern Sculpture From Rodin to 1969*, Baltimore Museum of Art, 1969.

ELSEN, ALBERT E., MCGOUGH, STEPHEN, and WANDER, STEVEN, *Rodin and Balzac*, Cantor, Fitzgerald, 1973.

ELSEN, ALBERT E., and MCNAMARA, MARY JO, *Rodin's Burghers of Calais*, Cantor, Fitzgerald, 1977.

GRAPPE, GEORGES, *Catalogue du Musée Rodin*, 1944. (Although dated, this is still a fundamental reference work for identifying and dating Rodin's work.)

SPEAR, ATHENA, *Rodin Sculptures in the Cleveland Museum of Art*, 1967; *A Supplement to Rodin Sculptures in the Cleveland Museum*, 1974.

TANCOCK, JOHN, *The Sculptures of Auguste Rodin, the Collection of the Rodin Museum in Philadelphia*, Philadelphia Museum of Art, 1976. (An exemplary catalogue of a great collection.)

THORSON, VICTORIA, *Rodin's Graphics*, California Palace of the Legion of Honor, 1975. (The best compilation of the graphics and their study.)

In recent years the Musée Rodin under the direction of Madame Monique Laurent has begun to publish a series of serious and important catalogues, of which the first three are:

LAURENT, MONIQUE, and JOUDRIN, CLAUDIE, *Rodin et les écrivains de son temps*, 1976.

LAURENT, MONIQUE, JOUDRIN, CLAUDIE, and VIÉVILLE, DOMINIQUE, *Rodin: le monument des*

Bourgeois de Calais (1884–1895) dans les collections du Musée Rodin et du Musée des Beaux-Arts, Calais, 1978.

LAURENT, MONIQUE, and JOUDRIN, CLAUDIE, *Rodin et l'Extrême-Orient*, 1979.

Important essays

BARTLETT, TRUMAN H., 'Auguste Rodin, Sculptor', a series of articles published in *American Architecture and Building News* in 1889 and reprinted in Elsen, Albert, *Auguste Rodin: Readings on His Life and Work*, Prentice Hall, 1965.

RILKE, RAINER MARIA, 'Auguste Rodin', written in 1903 and reproduced in Elsen, *Auguste Rodin: Readings on His Life and Work*. Translation by Jessie Lamont and Hans Trausil. This is one of the greatest essays written on the artist and exerted considerable influence on the way Europeans viewed Rodin's work.

SIMMEL, GEORGES, 'L'Oeuvre de Rodin comme expression de l'esprit moderne', in his *Mélange des philosophies relativiste*, Alcan, 1912.

STEINBERG, LEO, 'Rodin', in *Other Criteria: Confrontations with Twentieth Century Art*, Oxford, 1972. (This essay ranks with Rilke's among the very best writings on Rodin.)

TYLER, PARKER, 'Rodin and Freud, Masters of Ambivalence', *Art News*, March, 1955.

Rodin's views on art

WERNER, ALFRED (Preface by), *On Art and Artists*, Peter Owen, 1958, translation by Mrs Romilly Fedden from Rodin's conversations with Paul Gsell.

DUJARDIN-BEAUMETZ, HENRI-CHARLES-ÉTIENNE, 'Conversations with Rodin', reproduced in Elsen, *Auguste Rodin: Readings on His Life and Work*. These conversations were first published in 1913. The translation was by Ann McGarrell.

RODIN, AUGUSTE, *Cathedrals of France*, English translation by Elizabeth Chase Geissbuhler, Beacon Press, 1965.

Books on Rodin

ELSEN, ALBERT E., *Rodin's Gates of Hell*, University of Minnesota Press, 1960. (This book is in the process of being revised and updated.)

ELSEN, ALBERT E., *Rodin*, Museum of Modern Art, 1963.

ELSEN, ALBERT E., and VARNEDOE, J. KIRK T., *The Drawings of Rodin*, Praeger, 1971. Additional contributions by Victoria Thorson and Elizabeth Chase Geissbuhler. Varnedoe's chronology of the drawings and identification of Rodin's forgers are basic to these subjects.

GEFFROY, GUSTAVE, *A. Rodin*, Dentu, 1892.

RILKE, RAINER M., *Lettres à Rodin*, preface by Georges Grappe, Émile Paul, 1931.

SCHMOLL, GEN. EISENWERTH, JOSEF ADOLF, *Der Torso also Symbol und Form*, Bruno Grimm, 1954. (This work contains important ideas about Rodin's partial figures.)

TUCKER, WILLIAM, *The Language of Sculpture*, Thames and Hudson, 1974. (The sections on Rodin constitute a provocative formalist reading with which I do not agree.)

More detailed bibliographies are given in Tancock's *The Sculptures of Auguste Rodin* and Descharnes and Chabrun's *Auguste Rodin*.

Index

NOTE: Figures in **bold** refer to Plate numbers

A. Works by Rodin